Criticism
and
Objectivity

RAMAN SELDEN

London
GEORGE ALLEN & UNWIN
Boston   Sydney

George Allen & Unwin (Publishers) Ltd,
40 Museum Street, London WC1A 1LU, UK

George Allen & Unwin (Publishers) Ltd,
Park Lane, Hemel Hempstead, Herts HP2 4TE, UK

Allen & Unwin, Inc.,
9 Winchester Terrace, Winchester, Mass. 01890, USA

George Allen & Unwin Australia Pty Ltd,
8 Napier Street, North Sydney, NSW 2060, Australia

First published in 1984

British Library Cataloguing in Publication Data

Selden, Raman
  Criticism and objectivity.
1. Criticism
I. Title
801'.95   PN81
ISBN 0-04-800023-X

Library of Congress Cataloging in Publication Data

Selden, Raman.
  Criticism and objectivity.
Bibliography: p.
Includes index.
1. Criticism. 2. Knowledge, Theory of. I. Title.
PN81.S364   1984   801'.95   83-22397
ISBN 0-04-800023-X

Set in 10 on 12 point Plantin by Setrite Typesetters
and printed in Great Britain
by Biddles Ltd, Guildford, Surrey

Contents

Acknowledgements

I would like to thank *Durham University Journal* for permission to use material from my article 'The reader and the text' (vol. 74, 1982, pp. 269–74) and the University of Essex for permission to use material from my 'Russian Formalism and Marxism: an unconcluded debate' (in *Literature, Society and the Sociology of Literature*, ed. F. Barker *et al.*, 1977, pp. 93–104).

I gratefully acknowledge the advice and encouragement I have received from Neil Hertz and Terry Eagleton. I am especially indebted to Ben Knights who read through the entire manuscript and made valuable suggestions.

TO JANE

Of course, with the exception of those who are content with themselves as forming the entire universe, solitary amid nothing, everyone wants to struggle back to some sort of objectivist position.

A. N. Whitehead

1

Introduction: the Edge of the Abyss

The title of this book arose as a reaction to reading David Bleich's *Subjective Criticism* (1978). It seemed to me that I wanted to deny all the assumptions and leanings of this carefully written work. Here are some of the sentences which drew out the spirit of contradiction most forcefully:

> The teaching of language and literature often boils down to simple supervision of natural growth processes. (p. 7)
>
> The objective paradigm requires that reality exist without contradiction. (p. 19)
>
> When we become aware that a symbolic objectification system is unsatisfactory, we try to resymbolize or explain it. As Kuhn discusses, such explanation can actually change the object of attention. . . . The motive for such important changes grows from personal and communal subjectivity. (p. 66)
>
> The assumption derived from the objective paradigm that all observers have the same perceptual response to a symbolic object creates the illusion that the object is real and that its meaning must reside in it. (p. 98)
>
> The activity of developing knowledge is as phylogenetically founded as the formation of new families. (p. 133)

The 'objective paradigm' which haunts the pages of Bleich's book is a curious dinosaur, a pre-Einsteinian breed of scientific positivism. I had believed for some time that many important contributors to the philosophy of science, and to historical and cultural studies, were attempting to redefine the meaning of objectivity, science and knowledge, with a view to overcoming the obstructions presented by nineteenth-century science. Their arguments for the non-commensurability of theories, the decentredness of the subject, and the plurality of viewpoints, do not commit us to a subjectivisation of knowledge of the kind envisaged by Bleich.

The polarisation of subjective and objective paradigms is part of the problem. The epistemological arguments have been well rehearsed. We may orient the subject–object polarity in one direction or another. The neo-Kantians and the followers of Heidegger and Husserl have taken a subjective trajectory, while the Marxists and some structuralists have presupposed the objectivity of structures. In the end, the terms 'objective' and 'subjective' appear to mark a *commitment* to a general view of knowledge. I decided to pin my flag to the mast and declare my allegiance to the objective paradigm. At the same time, I was aware, in reading Bleich, that many of his objections to the objective paradigm as he conceived it were correct, but that they could just as easily be invoked in support of a differently conceived objective paradigm. In this spirit I have attempted to assimilate some aspects of structuralism, post-structuralism, reception aesthetics and other movements which have theorised subjectivity and the role of reader, to a historical criticism, which is committed to an objective paradigm; that is, to the possibility of an objective knowledge of the historical determinants of literary texts. This knowledge includes an explanation of the plural meaning of texts both from the point of view of their production and reception.

On the face of it (and perhaps beneath), this is a reactionary enterprise. Surely the future lies with such exciting experimental criticism as Bernard Sharratt's brilliant *Reading Relations* (1982)? I would suggest, on the contrary, that a convincing historical and objective criticism has not been allowed time to develop. In England, following the influx of continental Marxist and structuralist texts at the end of the 1960s, important books were written by Terry Eagleton (*Criticism and Ideology*, 1976) and Raymond Williams (*The Country and the City*, 1976), a series of literature and society conferences were held at Essex University, and a series of valuable 'Working Papers' were issued by the Cultural Studies Centre at Birmingham. However, before these developments could be assimilated, we were overtaken by the radical deconstructive movement led by the followers of Lacan and Derrida. The interesting symbiosis of Marxism, Lacanian psychoanalysis and Derridian deconstruction has, in my view, come up against a series of dead ends. By retracing the steps not in a simple ahistorical reaction but through the defiles of a necessarily changed problematic, I wish to regain the footing which has been denied to the historical critic by the incisive acid of deconstruction.

Among the formidable philosophical objections to my project from a post-structuralist viewpoint, the most powerful would be those concerning metalanguages. A metalanguage is a discourse which is set to work upon another discourse. For the post-structuralist there can be no metalinguistic vantage point, no authoritative grounding for our critical discourse. The critic can only cover one discourse with another; he or she cannot dis-cover. In *S/Z* (1975), Barthes conceives his own metalanguage (the 'codes') not as a conceptual apparatus capable of disclosing structures, but as a network of voices off which echo in the text:

> Hence we use *Code* here not in the sense of a list, a paradigm that must be reconstituted. The code is a perspective of quotations, a mirage of structures; we know only its departures and returns ... they are so many fragments of something that has always been *already* read, seen, done, experienced. ... Or again: each code is one of the forces that can take over the text (of which the text is the network), one of the voices out of which the text is woven. (Barthes, 1975, pp. 20–1)

On this view, criticism cannot be a metalanguage. What he prefers to call 'textual analysis' is itself merely another text and can never be a commentary:

> The subject of the analysis (the critic, the philologist, the scholar) cannot in fact, without bad faith and smugness, believe he is external to the language he is describing. His exteriority is only quite provisional and apparent: he too is in language, and he must assume his insertion, however 'rigorous' and 'objective' he may wish to be, into the triple knot of the subject, the signifier, and the Other – an insertion which writing (the text) fully accomplishes, without having recourse to the hypocritical distance of a fallacious metalanguage. (Young, p. 44)

We are presented here with that strange determinism of indeterminacy which produces in us an intolerable vertigo. The 'triple knot' (subject/signifier/Other) appears to centre itself, so to speak, in the dominance of the signifier. The subject of discourse is 'always a fading thing that runs under the chain of signifiers' (Macksey and Donato, p. 194), and itself becomes a signifier in the linguistic system in its subjection to the Other. If we say that what we have called criticism is the pursuit of the signifier in search of the signified, then the search is doomed to failure: we will never catch up with the signifier, and never drive it to its signified.

The post-structuralists themselves are, inevitably, caught in the same dizzying dilemma. A classic demonstration is Barbara Johnson's discussion of Derrida's reading of Lacan's reading of Poe's story 'The Purloined Letter'. Lacan reads the story as an allegory of the signifier. In Derrida's view, Lacan's essay affirms the absolute truth of psychoanalytic theories and the absolute decipherability of the literary text. However, Barbara Johnson argues that Derrida consistently forces Lacan's statements into systems and patterns from which they are actually trying to escape; Lacan's text is itself more indeterminate and problematic than the received Lacanian psychoanalysis would allow. Paradoxically, both Lacan and Derrida, *against their wills*, allow 'slipping from the signifier to the signified'. She concludes that the readings enact 'the impossibility of any ultimate analytic metalanguage, the eternal oscillation between unequivocal undecidability and ambiguous certainty' (Young, p. 242). Reading, it seems, is always misreading. All reading is a rewriting, which insists on a signified. The text which is read always exceeds the reading. There are, however, two ways of viewing this relentless asymmetry. Barbara Johnson appears to believe that while reading cannot avoid metalinguistic assertions, the text always says more, and it is that 'more' which tells of the primacy of the signifier. On the other hand, that two masters of post-structuralism should be driven to discover signifieds might carry another lesson. The principal sin of reading is the repression of the signifier, the denial of the text's pleasure. But we might more justly regard a purely ludic reading as a ludicrous desire to return to that polymorphous, pre-symbolic state which Kristeva and others regard as the truly un-repressed moment when the biophysical drives traverse the infant's body in a disordered profusion. We are faced by a myth of primitivism, it appears, a version of the old culture–nature contention.

The joining of signifier and signified in reading is the very process of 'intending' a meaning and 'understanding' a meaning. The post-structuralists dissolve metalanguage into the infinite infernal lake of 'writing' and thereby untie the knots of intention, meaning, concept, model and finally science.

Gayatri Spivak has given us a useful account of the 'double bind' of the deconstructive movement:

> Deconstruction seems to offer a way out of the closure of knowledge. By inaugurating the open-ended indefiniteness of textuality – by thus 'placing in the abyss' (*mettre en abime*)...it shows us the lure of the abyss as freedom.... We are intoxicated with the prospect of never hitting bottom.
>
> Thus a further deconstruction deconstructs deconstruction, both as the search for a foundation (the critic behaving as if she means what she says in her text), and as the pleasure of the bottomless. (Spivak, p. lxxvii)

From the point of view of a Marxist criticism, there is no pleasure in the prospect of never hitting bottom; as a theory of history, Marxism discovers its ultimate footing beneath the level of the textual in the socio-economic. Two aspects of post-structuralism are especially inimical to a Marxist position: the theory of signification and the theory of the 'subject'. Both history and the 'subject' are seen as products of signifying practices. From this point of view, Marxist history is merely the privileging of a set of rhetorical strategies, involving models, binary systems and metaphors. Some Marxists have tried to argue that, since signification enters as an element in all social practices, we should simply redefine the Marxist concept of social formation as a nexus of discursive practices. Similarly, attempts have been made to insert the Lacanian 'subject' into the Marxist theory of ideology (Coward and Ellis). These approaches run up against the essential features of a Marxist histori-cal theory: individual agents are in some sense 'bearers' of subject positions within a set of social relations and ideological discourses; discourses are articulated *in* social formations and do not themselves constitute social formations (Adlam *et al.*; Hall).

Michel Foucault's later work has concentrated on the theme of

discursive *power* (see Sheridan, pp. 113-34). While he resembles
Derrida and Lacan in accepting the decentering of the subject and
the relativisation of 'truth', Foucault preserves from his earlier work
a distinctive emphasis on the *historicity* of discourses. He does not
conceive the history of discourses as the endless reinscription of a
general text, and insists on their discontinuity, emergence and
reversal in the course of a historical power struggle. The Nietzschean
'will to knowledge', which underlies this highly political theory, is a
rancorous and destructive instinct which tries to govern discourse by
prohibitions, exclusions and limitations. Foucault places special
emphasis upon the institutional basis of this process of struggle. The
work of a scientist, for example, is recognised as 'true' only if it falls
within the prescribed boundaries of truth as defined by the dis-
ciplinary consensus, organs of learning, and institutional authorities,
which make up the discursive formation of his or her time. It is not
enough to speak the truth, one must be 'in the truth' (*dans le vrai*)
(Foucault, 1972, p. 224). Nevertheless, one must add that it is
indeed possible to speak the truth but not to be in the truth. Mendel,
Foucault himself pointed out, spoke the truth 'in a void' during the
1860s (p. 224). Foucault's concern to speak of the 'political
economy' of truth seems to forbid any distinction between 'knowledge' and 'ideology'.

However, by placing on the agenda what he calls 'effective
history', by admitting the possibility that the historian (pre-eminently
Foucault) seeks to trace the changes in discursive formations and to
note the moments of usurpation or appropriation of discourse, he
effectively recognises the field of a knowledge. Then, like the other
post-structuralists he corrects this tilt by insisting that all knowledge
is perspective: we can never stand outside the discursive formation
which is the ground of our knowledge. Frank Lentricchia has very
wisely pointed out that the necessarily historicised position of the
historian (as understood by Foucault) is not a 'bar to historical study,
but its very condition' (p. 207). He further suggests that 'the historical consciousness, the will to knowledge itself, though it can never be
neutralized, is itself open to historical exploration and at least partial
definition' (p. 207). For many post-structuralists the only good text
is one which wrings its own neck or, as Culler puts it, 'The value and
force of a text may depend to a considerable extent on the way it
deconstructs the philosophy that subtends it' (Culler, 1983, p. 98).

However, while knowledge may be implicated in power and subject to discursive forces, it may also possess its own specific effectivity. Mendel's science eventually became situated 'in the truth' (although its location in the power system of knowledge can never be guaranteed), but not merely as the result of a successful power struggle. Foucault's own historical studies of penal, medical and sexual history have an explanatory power which would not be nullified in a hostile discursive formation. If, like Mendel's genetics, Foucault's 'genealogies' of discourse had been produced 'in a void', their ultimate entry into 'truth' would have been inevitable. This is not true in the case of the genetics of Lysenko (see Chapter 3) whose 'science' was constituted as knowledge only when it was transformed by ideology (see Lecourt).

Foucault's (and Edward Said's) view of discursive practice extends the perspective of post-structuralism towards a *praxis*: the deconstructing of the rhetorical and metaphoric strategies of specific discourses is conducted as a political act, as an intervention in a power struggle. Christopher Norris believes that the Nietzschean side of Foucault's project succeeds in supplanting the Marxian paradigm of knowledge:

> History writing on Nietzschean terms involves a surrender of the privileged claim to knowledge once entertained by the sovereign consciousness.... Foucault follows Nietzsche in deconstructing those systems of thought which mask their incessant will to power behind a semblance of objective knowledge. (Norris, pp. 86, 87)

Norris's argument follows the implacable logic of deconstruction, which removes the ground of each knowledge by exposing (deconstructing) the rhetorical strategies and metaphorical 'ruses' which constitute it. His apparent acceptance of Foucault's and Said's interventionism in no way dilutes his rigorous textualising of history and knowledge. He concludes that 'Only by following through the logic of deconstruction, rather than meeting its challenge halfway, can thought escape this imprisonment by the metaphors of its own frozen discourse. Nietzsche remains at the last a disturbing threat to the "taken-for-granted" rhetoric of Marxist theory' (Norris, p. 89). I do not deny the omnipresence of rhetorical strategies in paradigms of knowledge. However, the assumption that knowledge is thereby totally relativised and that only power determines its validity seems to me highly questionable.

If one returns to the fountain-head of deconstructive logic (I humbly erase my allusion to origins) in *The Will to Power*, the enormous gulf between a Marxian and a Nietzschean praxis becomes apparent:

> To introduce a meaning – this task still remains to be done, assuming there is no meaning yet. Thus it is with sounds, but also with the fate of peoples: they are capable of the most different interpretations and direction toward different goals.
>
> On a yet higher level is to *posit a goal* and mould facts according to it; that is, active interpretation and not merely conceptual translation.
>
> Ultimately, man finds in things nothing but what he himself has imported into them: the finding is called science, the importing – art, religion, love, pride. Even if this should be a piece of childishness, one should carry on with both and be well disposed toward both – some should find; others – *we* others! – should import! (Nietzsche, p. 327)

The subordination of science to ideology, the perverse celebration of the will to knowledge/power, and the thoroughgoing scepticism, are the recurring preoccupations of modern post-structuralism.

Another ploy of the deconstructor is to displace a binary opposition which is seen as the rhetorical underpinning of an entire problematic. The opposition between self and world, for example, has been regarded by some modern critics as a necessary fiction for a whole range of humanistic and deterministic philosophies. Invoking C. S. Peirce's critique of Descartes, Walter Benn Michaels argues that both the subjectivist and objectivist perspectives on interpretation are invalid:

> In rejecting the Cartesian goal of neutrality, he [Peirce] rejects on the one hand a notion of the self free to assert its subjectivity without constraint and on the other hand a notion of the self wiped clean of prejudice and ready to accept determinate

meaning. . . . The self, like the world, is a text. Hence the notion of an autonomous unconstituted subject is just as problematic (and for the same reasons) as the autonomous and unconstituted world. (Michaels, pp. 198–9)

This position has considerable force. The notions of the self as 'free' or 'wiped clean of prejudice' are also questionable from the viewpoint of historical materialism. Marxist critiques of 'idealism' and 'empiricism' have traversed similar ground. However, the claim (essential to all post-structuralist theories) that 'The self, like the world, is a text' is completely at odds with any claim of historical *knowledge*. Any knowledge, it appears, is necessarily self-defeating, since it is implicated in the discursive forces it employs to articulate itself. This too, one should note, involves a presupposition of the textuality of both the subject and the world. The history of science suggests that knowledge is not something which arises when a neutral subject reflects upon an unconstituted world, but rather when there occurs an abrupt replacement of a whole structure of problems and concepts by another set. One must accept that knowledge is always subject to struggle, that scientific concepts are discursive strategies, and that a belief in absolute knowledge, whether empiricist or idealist, is an illusion. However, a knowledge effect is not chimerical: an adjustment takes place not merely within discourse, but also in our relationship to the world. The adjustments between social agents, discourse and world are not simply the effects of a power struggle *within* discourse. There *is* a power struggle, but it is articulated within the field of forces and conditions which limit and, in a decentred fashion, determine its possibilities. Foucault conceives all historical conditions of discourses as being marshalled in support of one side or another in a power struggle for access to the throne of 'truth'. This politicisation of knowledge reduces history to a gladiatorial arena in which *epistemes* fight it out. The collapsing of 'self' and 'world' into 'discourse' lays an ancient ghost of epistemology but raises ontological problems which won't lie down.

I am proposing an objectivist position which recognises, on the one hand, the multivalence of discourse and, on the other, the validity of metalingual operations. At a basic textual level, Jakobson argued that metalanguage is an essential feature of interpretive discourse. Consider his example:

When the universe of discourse prompts a technological nomenclature, *dog* is sensed as a name of various gripping and holding tools, while *horse* designates various supportive devices. In Russian *kon'ki* 'little horses' became a name of skates. Two contiguous stanzas of Pushkin's *Eugène Onegin* . . . depict the country in early winter, and the gaiety of the little peasant boys cutting the new ice with their skates (little horses) is confronted with the tedious time of the landlord whose helpless saddle horse stumbles over the ice. The poet's clear-cut contrastive parallelism of *kon'ki* and *kon'* 'horse' gets lost in translation into languages without the equine image of the skates. The conversion of *kon'ki* from animals into inanimate tools of locomotion, with a corresponding change in the declensional paradigm, has been effected under a metalingual control. (Jakobson, p. 91)

Such control insists on limiting connotation according to determinate contexts. It is true that the introduction or repression of connotations cannot be outlawed by the controls of metalanguage, and consequently there can be no authoritative interpretation. However, by establishing the determinate elements in a field of discourse, we have at least a basis for understanding the semantic potentiality of the text. A reader of the Pushkin stanzas who repressed or ignored the verbal play would be 'misreading' in a more determinate sense than some deconstructors would acknowledge. Any adequate theory of reading must take account of misreading and be able to theorise both a text's potential readings and its possible 'misreadings'. When applied to poetic work, 'misreading' takes on quite positive connotations. According to Harold Bloom, all 'strong' poets, eager to throw off the anxiety of influence, and to establish their own identity, are compelled to misread their poetic fathers by 'troping' them and thereby displacing their poetic meaning. Readers too misread in this sense. Of course, such a concept of misreading presupposes a relatively determinate discourse which is displaced.

We are left with the question, 'Is there a historical criticism which can survive the deconstructive gaze?' Like Foucault, Derrida insists upon the historicity of discourse: all meanings, all readings, and all texts are subject to the historical process of reinscription. He adds, to our discomfort, that a 'historical approach' cannot limit a text's meanings by appealing to historical determinants of meaning. Culler summarises this argument lucidly:

> A 'historical approach' appeals to historical narratives – stories of changes in thinking and of the thoughts or beliefs appropriate to distinguishable historical periods – in order to control the meaning of rich and complex works by ruling out possible meanings as historically inappropriate. These historical narratives are produced by interpreting the supposedly less complex and ambiguous texts of a period, and their authority to authorize or control meanings of the most complex texts is certainly questionable. The history invoked as ultimate reality and source of truth manifests itself in narrative constructs, stories designed to yield meaning through narrative ordering. (Culler, 1983, p. 129)

One can accept that 'rich and complex works' are not reducible to the dominant ideology ('thoughts or beliefs') of their period. No history of ideas could provide an adequate matrix for the generation of textual meaning. On the other hand, one cannot accept the *textualisation* of history. The point about history as 'narrative constructs' resembles Hayden White's in *Tropics of Discourse* in which he reduces all history writing to certain 'master tropes' (metaphor, metonymy, synecdoche and irony), and argues that discourse establishes its adequacy to the objects it addresses 'by a *pre*-figurative move that is more tropical than logical' (p. 1). If we reduce history writing to a rhetorical manoeuvre, we can no longer ask questions about conceptual adequacy. Figurative language, it is true, is inseparable from conceptual thought in all types of knowledge. When scientists cannot explain a process, they construct models. Darwin, not being able to explain the process by which changes occur in animals and plants in nature, constructed a model which involved a comparison between the known processes of breeding and selection of domestic animals with the unknown processes in nature. The model was elaborated by borrowing from Malthus's population theory. It has become usual to forget the figurative construction of Darwin's theory of natural selection. By deconstructing it, we may gain an understanding of Darwin's theoretical labour, but the issue of conceptual adequacy remains open, and is not determined with reference only to the rhetorical level of the theory.

It is not surprising that many of these problems have been debated among Marxists, since for them knowledge of history is fundamental. The work of Louis Althusser has never entered the main stream of historical studies in this country. The leading figures in the Marxist tradition, especially Raymond Williams and E. P. Thompson, have remained unreceptive (in Thompson's case hostile) to Althusser's version of Marx's theory of history, which is inimical to their native English empiricism, their Leavisian commitment to the (to them) fundamental category of 'experience'. The great value of the work done by these English socialist historians has been fully acknowledged by another fine Marxist historian, Perry Anderson, whose work was deeply influenced by Althusser (Anderson, 1980). There are serious shortcomings in Althusser's work, as Anderson has himself deftly shown (1976, pp. 64–6; 1980, pp. 75–9). Nevertheless, there remain certain clarifications and reformulations of the Marxist theory of history which are of immense value to all historians, not least literary historians.

The concept of 'social formation' had very little currency in Marxist writings before Althusser. It replaces the term 'society' for vital strategic reasons: 'society' tends to denote a unitary social bloc or complexly functioning totality. Althusser's 'social formation' is conceptually divided into three regions – economic, political and ideological. Human practices may be theorised as occurring in one or other region. Historical study involves understanding of the 'specific effectivity' of practices (their non-reducible features), the uneven development of regions in historical time, the structure of determinations which characterise specific social formations, and the mechanisms of crisis or revolution. The significance of Althusser's work for literary studies attaches especially to his general characterisation of the formation, which as Perry Anderson points out 'was initially introduced as a forcible reminder that the diversity of human practices in any society is irreducible to economic practice alone' (Anderson, 1980, p. 68). It is important to note that the *analytic* distinction between various levels in a social formation does not entail a belief in the *separate* existence of different objective practices. To ignore this would, of course, sanction a formalistic

approach to the study of particular regional practices (such as literature, religion, law, economy).

The 'historical approach' to literary studies is a term which covers
a multitude of sins. I do not propose to speak for the prosecution or
the defence. Instead, I would like to advocate an approach to
historical criticism which avoids both the totalising metaphysics of a
geisteswissenschaft and the forms of determinism which deny literary
discourse its proper degree of autonomy. In my view, even if one can
construct an adequate model of the historical conditions which
subtend specific texts, the 'geometry' of the relations between
conditions and texts cannot be described so as to produce a single
determinate meaning. This is so, partly because texts are 'overdetermined' and partly because, whatever a text's conditions of production may be, its reception is also located in history. The recent vogue
for reader-response criticism does not acknowledge the distinction
between production and reception, since it assumes that all claims to
knowledge or interpretive validity are simply variations of response.
The difficulties of sustaining the distinction are considerable in the
face of semiotic, psychoanalytic and deconstructive attacks on the
concept of historical knowledge. The reader of this book will notice
that as it proceeds it moves into deeper entanglement with the post-
structuralist problematic. It may even appear that the pass has been
sold or abandoned in the final chapter. However, a more adequate
historical criticism can, perhaps, arise only on the very edge of the
abyss which beckons the critic's halting steps. In Chapters 2, 3 and 4,
I stand on safe ground, ignoring the siren calls from the abyss; in
Chapter 5, I move within earshot but refuse to take heed; in Chapters 6
and especially 7, I camp on the margins of deconstruction. I greet the
reader there in the belief that survival is possible, but perhaps I am
not waving but drowning.

2

Objectivity and Theory in English Criticism

The view that there is no fact of the matter as to whether or not things are good or bad or better or worse, etc. has, in a sense, become institutionalised. (Putnam, p. 128)

English criticism since Wordsworth has been unable to rid itself of an unsatisfactory theory of the emotions, with the result that the 'irrational' element in both art and criticism has assumed a false preponderance. (Casey, p. xi)

Since the seventeenth century most influential English critics have anchored their speculations to the firm sea-bed of empiricism. Their critical practices have often taken the forms of pragmatic, moralistic or affective commentary. Dr Johnson, for example, was fond of applying his sceptical view of human reason to the activities of critics. His remarks on works of literary appreciation still find an echo in the hearts of many English academics:

There are few books on which more time is spent by young students, than on treatises which deliver the characters of authors; nor any which oftener deceive the expectation of the reader, or fill his mind with more opinions which the progress of his studies and the encrease of his knowledge oblige him to resign. (*Rambler*, no. 93, 1751, Johnson, Vol. 4, p. 130)

Any attempt to do more than 'transmit the general suffrage of mankind' is grandly dismissed as a manifestation of literary prejudice or of 'the refinements of subtilty and the dogmatism of learning'. Common sense and experience are eternally on the alert against the insidious temptations of opinion and arrogant theory:

'Life is not the object of science: we see a little, very little' (*Adventurer*, no. 107, 1753, Johnson, Vol. 2, p. 445). The Baconian appeal to a democracy of common sense has certainly had its salutary effects in protecting criticism from inbreeding, but this healthy scepticism about theory has always tended to become a reactionary and self-destructive cynicism.

The Romantic poets and critics, following Kant and Hegel, placed 'art' in a new position of significance in human life: poetry offered insights into 'truth', an access to experiences which could not be afforded by philosophy, science or even religion. But the advance in status was achieved at a price. Unlike German Romanticism, English Romanticism was almost exclusively confined to the arts; there was no English Hegel (Coleridge as philosopher still has the appearance of an exotic growth). During the eighteenth century, the trend in aesthetics and criticism which has been dubbed 'pre-Romantic' developed its principles of judgement on the basis of an opposition between poetry of reason and poetry of genius. Joseph Warton's elevation of Milton at the expense of Pope prepared the way for a deeper dichotomy in the Romantic period between poetry and science. While Wordsworth attempted to establish a noble synthesis ('Poetry is the breath and finer spirit of all knowledge; the impassioned expression which is in the Countenance of all Science'), the Romantic period is marked by an extreme contradiction between its aesthetic and its socio-economic ideologies: the idealist bent of Romantic poetry is brutally contradicted by the hard-headed calculations of Bentham and James Mill.

J. S. Mill's wish to overcome the split between thought and feeling in his own life has a larger significance and influence in the nineteenth century. His tribute to Wordsworth is well known: 'What made Wordsworth's poems a medicine for my state of mind, was that they expressed, not merely outward beauty, but states of feeling . . . under the excitement of beauty. They seemed the very culture of the feelings, which I was in quest of.' (Mill, 1969, p. 89) A. N. Whitehead argued that Wordsworth had healed a split between fact and value which had developed in the late seventeenth century and had been formulated philosophically in Locke's distinction between primary and secondary qualities. Whitehead invokes romantic poetry in support of his organic conception of nature: 'the nature-poetry of the romantic revival was a protest on behalf of the organic

view of nature, and also a protest against the exclusion of value from
the essence of matter of fact.' (Whitehead, p. 133) However, it is not
clear that Wordsworth overcame the fact–value dichotomy in his
response to science. On the one hand, like earlier German writers
(see Lillian R. Furst's discussion of Franz von Baader, p. 139),
Coleridge and Shelley, he regarded science and philosophy as
imaginative apprehensions of the underlying unity of the universe
(poetry is 'in the countenance of all Science'). On the other hand, his
writings stand as a radical rejection of contemporary mechanical
materialism, the received Newtonian universe of dead matter. However, the underlying associationist bent of his poetry and thought
should never be overlooked. H. W. Garrod's remarks on
Wordsworth's major poetry (to 1807) still carry conviction:

> the mysticism of Wordsworth is grounded and rooted, actually,
> *in* the senses. The natural world speaks, not to the intellect,
> but to that which is most 'natural', viz. our senses. This pure
> sensationalism of Wordsworth . . . is apt to take us by surprise.
> (Garrod, pp. 105–6)

Whitehead is attracted especially by Wordsworth's anti-abstractionism; great poets, says Whitehead, 'express deep intuitions of mankind penetrating into what is universal in concrete fact' (p. 122).
Wordsworth begins by accepting the 'obstinate irreducible, matter-
of-fact entities' as the limiting domain of reality. This insistence on
the 'concrete' as the bedrock of cognition preserves a connecting link
between empiricism, intuitionism and nature mysticism. The
Cartesian body–mind dichotomy, which lies at the heart of the
fact–value opposition, is not transcended in Wordsworth's critical
writings. His emphasis on the poet's developed *sensibility* makes
problematic the grandiose cognitive claims for poetry. In 'Essay,
Supplementary to the Preface' (1815), he tones down these claims:
'The appropriate business of poetry . . ., her privilege and her *duty*,
is to treat of things not as they *are*, but as they *seem* to exist to the
senses, and to the passions.' The dichotomy between subject and
object, denied so firmly by Coleridge, is here strongly stated.

Mill's restatement of Wordsworth's 1800 Preface elaborates and
deepens the science–poetry opposition:

> The object of poetry is confessedly to act upon the emotions; and therein is poetry sufficiently distinguished from what Wordsworth affirms to be its logical opposite; namely, not prose, but matter of fact or science. The one addresses itself to the belief; the other, to the feelings. The one does its work by convincing or persuading; the other, by offering interesting objects of contemplation to the sensibilities (*What is Poetry?*).

What is striking here, from a European perspective, is the characteristically British dichotomy. The German Romantics refuse to adopt such a simplifying polarity: Schiller, Hegel, Schelling and others insist on the dichotomy within reason itself, between a higher state (*Vernunft*) and a mere reflective reason or understanding (*Verstand*). Coleridge and Blake also avoid the oversimplification of cognition, but their solutions were too abstruse and un-English to filter into the dominant popular strain of Romantic ideology. Mill's writings on poetry show considerable subtlety and flexibility, but are founded on an unchanging empiricist epistemology which divides experience rigorously between inner and outer worlds, imagination and reason, feeling and thought:

> Whatever opinion we hold respecting the fundamental identity or diversity of matter and mind, in any case the distinction between mental and physical facts, between the internal and the external world, will always remain as a matter of classification. (Mill, 1965, p. 24)

The demands of reasons are counterbalanced by the authority of inner culture of the feelings. His stress upon the need for a symbiotic and harmonious relationship between the two spheres conceals his ultimate commitment to the cognitive authority of science. Indeed in his 1835 essay on Tennyson, the limitations of poetry are underlined when he refers to:

> an error to which the philosophical speculations of poets are peculiarly liable – that of embracing as truth, not the conclusions which are recommended by the strongest evidence, but those which have the most poetical appearance. (Mill, 1981, p. 417)

Mill argues that, whatever 'philosophical system' a poet adopts, the materials of all poetry consists of 'human feelings'. However, by attending to the dictates of 'impartial reason', the poet will achieve truth and not merely beauty:

> Whoever, in the greatest concerns of human life, pursues truth with unbiassed feelings, and an intellect adequate to discern it will not find the resources of poetry are lost to him because he has learnt to use, and not to abuse them. (Mill, 1981, p. 417)

Mill's synthetic cast of mind is reflected in the pairing of 'unbiassed feelings' and 'adequate' intellect; he might, more naturally, have reversed the epithets. This fudging of the dichotomy is of great importance to his aesthetic ideology. The separation of fact and value is felt to be unsatisfactory but inescapable, and therefore, even while healing the breach between thought and feeling, Mill preserves the dichotomy between emotive and factual discourses.

At their worst, Mill's critical writings highlight the dangers of a naïvely affective approach. His discussion of R. M. Milnes's poems (1838) is especially revealing. Mill discloses disarmingly his political sympathy with Milnes, 'a young and active' MP who 'generally votes with the Tories' and belongs to the pro-Church and aristocratic 'Coleridgian reaction'. 'With Conservatives of this description, however we may doubt the practicability of their objects, we feel, and have always professed, the most entire sympathy.' (Mill, 1981, p. 510) His discussion of Milnes's poems is of a piece with his affective endorsement of the politics. The appalling sub-Wordsworthian 'Lay of the Humble' is narrated by a persona who expresses the platitudes dear to the heart of the paternalistic Toryism half-admired by Mill:

> Thus without share in coin or land,
> But well content to hold
> The wealth of nature in my hand.

Mill's comments, with their stress on intuitive response, sincerity and affective essence, are shockingly inappropriate to the poem in hand:

This poem requires no commentator; it goes straight to the common heart of humanity; and we shall be surprised if it does not become widely known. . . . The man who can thus write, is entitled to write in verse. . . . Let such a man speak from the fulness of his own heart – give him thoughts and feelings to express which are deeply interesting to him – and it will be a little your own fault if he does not make them interesting to you. Now these poems, as a whole, if there be faith in internal evidence, do come from the heart of the writer; what they express, he feels, or has felt; they are the deepest and most earnest part of himself, thrown into melodious language; there is as much sincerity in them as there can be in words; for properly speaking, it is only a man's whole life which is sincere – *that* alone is the utterance of the whole man, contemplative and active taken together. (Mill, 1981, p. 509)

Mill here effaces both the critic (the poem 'requires no commentator') and the object of criticism ('words'); we are left with the reader's 'inward evidence', the poet's 'whole life', and 'the common heart of humanity'.

I am suggesting that Mill's science–poetry dichotomy became the dominant critical paradigm of English criticism. His formulations and reformulations of Wordsworth's programmatic utterances fitted the empiricist cast of English culture far better than the German-inspired transcendental line of Coleridge and Carlyle. Mill's regard for Wordsworth was shared by many major writers of the nineteenth century; M. H. Abrams rightly claims that for the most sensitive critics in the generation or so after Wordsworth's death, it was precisely his extraordinary success in bringing consolation to a 'time of dereliction and dismay' that give him such stature. Arnold wrote of Wordsworth's 'healing power', Leslie Stephen believed that 'Wordsworth is the only poet who will bear reading in times of distress', and John Morley spoke of his ability 'to give us quietness' (see Abrams, p. 134). In the harsh world of Victorian capitalism, the Wordsworthian fusion of individual transcendence and experiential immediacy had a stronger appeal for critics than the more strident and embattled ethics of Carlyle or Ruskin.

It would be wrong to place all the English Romantics under the same general description. Lillian Furst rather misleadingly writes of European Romanticism in terms of a balance (a 'see-saw') of feeling and imagination. Giving due weight to the importance of imagination in German and some English Romantics, she is forced to generalise as follows: 'far from being primary, the expression of feeling is much rather the outcome of the individualism of the Romantic attitude' (Furst, p. 213). Only the French allowed feeling to predominate. This somewhat statistical approach is especially unhelpful in the case of English Romanticism. In view of the enormous social and ideological significance of the different emphases among writers, it is essential to avoid historicist period categories; the contradictions between Blake and Wordsworth, or Shelley and Byron, reflect important differences in these poets' responses to their historical situations. The predominance of the Wordsworthian synthesis is of great cultural moment. Yet, in one respect Furst's argument about feeling is correct. Mill's polarisation of science and poetry effaces the *cognitive* claims of poetry to a degree which marks a real break with even Wordsworth. Mill's 'Romanticism' is a subtle and perhaps unconscious assimilation of Romantic thought to a different system (see Carr).

A 'deconstructive' reading of Mill would be revealing. The antithesis, science and poetry, taken with his system of philosophy as a whole is hierarchised in favour of science. Even when he argues for a view of poetry as compensatory culture of the inner life, poetry remains secondary and requires a strengthening objectivity. It 'supplements' science, but is itself a lack. Mill's personal sense of the one-sided sterility of science threatened to subvert the cognitive priority of science, but in his reading of Tennyson he explicitly re-establishes a 'violent hierarchy'. The Romantic poets too grappled with the same intractable dichotomies, but often with greater insight.

Keats's ambiguous or vacillating uses of terms like 'truth', 'sensation' and 'thought' are the symptoms of a mind struggling seriously with the counter-claims of science and poetry. Neither his letters nor his best poetry embodies a simple opposition between the truths of the imagination and the truths of 'consecutive reason'. However, no nineteenth-century Romantic poet arrived at a position as subtle as the dialectical vision of the eighteenth-century William Blake, whose early work embodies an anthropocentric idealism which is unique in Romantic poetry. In Blake's poetry there is embedded an implicit theory of consciousness (usually dissipated in critical clichés about 'vision' and 'imagination') which overcomes the fact–value opposition. The subject–object division is transcended: Blake's 'vision' cuts across the 'inner' and 'outer' fields of Locke's perceptual model. It was of the utmost significance for English culture that Blake had no audience and no important heirs (until Yeats). J. S. Mill was able to embrace the palliative of Wordsworthian sublimity without dismantling his own empiricism.

The opposition between the languages of poetry and of science, between 'subjective' and 'objective' truths, persisted in English criticism, surviving notably in I. A. Richard's distinction between emotive and referential uses of language. Inevitably the separation was transferred to criticism itself. The wide acceptance of the 'empirical' procedures of New Criticism did little to erase a deep-seated assumption of the fundamentally intuitive and subjective nature of critical practice. Subjective response and theoretical proposition, evaluation and description, were fixed as alternative, essentially distinct aspects, of verbal procedure. The Romantic legacy leaves the critic a choice between, on one side, the importation of extra-literary 'objective' criteria (literary history, linguistics, philology, bibliography) and, on the other, the self-sufficiency of intuition and value judgement. We are left with an opposition between scholarship and criticism, science and humanism, fact and value.

Romantic anti-abstractionism, an outlook which marginalised Coleridge, and which links the Romantics to Dr Johnson, has been as important to modern English criticism as the related poetry–science antithesis. Hazlitt's opposition to Coleridge's metaphysical abstractness is representative of a more general and 'popular' Romanticism. Equally opposed to utilitarianism, he insisted on the fundamentally individual and intuitive nature of authentic perceptions. Women, he argued, 'are less implicated in theories; and judge of objects more from their immediate and involuntary impression on the mind, and, therefore, more truly and naturally' (Hazlitt, Vol. 8, p. 77). His English disdain for German criticism has all the amused superiority of Dr Johnson: they 'have no shades of opinion, but are always straining at a grand systematic conclusion. . . . No question can come before them but they have a large apparatus of logical and metaphysical principles ready to play off upon it' (Hazlitt, Vol. 16, p. 58). Reason is necessary to a critic, but 'his criticism must operate from a foundation in feeling'. The moral dimension of Hazlitt's outlook is evident in his comments on Joseph Fawcett: 'He was incapable of harbouring a sinister motive, and judged only from what he felt. There was no flaw or mist in the clear mirror of his mind. He was as open to impressions as he was strenuous in maintaining them' (Hazlitt, Vol. 8, pp. 224–5).

In England, moral criticism has remained dominant, and relentlessly anti-theoretical. Dr Johnson's particular stress on literature's 'imitation of life' and upon experience as the final arbiter in criticism has had a lasting influence. Interest in the autonomy of art has been a significant development in France (*l'art pour l'art* and *symbolisme*), in Germany (Kant), in America (Susanne Langer, Wallace Stevens, Northrop Frye), and in Eastern Europe (Russian Formalism, the Prague Circle), but not in England, where the critical tradition of Dr Johnson, Arnold and Leavis has proved the most vigorous and productive. The criteria of Leavis's criticism are located ambiguously between the internal structures of literature and the surrounding field of 'life'. There is no naïve subordination of art to life, no simple moral reductionism. But, as René Wellek once observed, Leavis's criteria remain inexplicit and unquestioned; there is an ultimate appeal to a shared socio-ethical response to literature which takes the place of a theoretical elaboration of underlying critical concepts (for his reply to Wellek, see Leavis, 1952, pp. 211–22). Leavis's concern to register an immediate 'felt' response led him to stop short of the explicit analysis of his own theoretical assumptions which he regarded as of less immediate concern. His position reflected confidence in a consensus of sensibility.

The underlying fact–value opposition, which was reinforced by the romantic distinction between the languages of science and poetry has continued to discourage the development of critical theory. The long-standing opposition between the words 'science' and 'values' requires that criticism should be a non-objective, non-rational activity.

The root of the problem, as John Casey admirably demonstrated, lies in certain preconceptions about the nature of language itself. Casey traces Wittgenstein's abandonment of his early 'picture theory' of language ('According to the picture theory the words in a sentence name elements in the world, and the form of the sentence bears a relation of logical analogy to the form of the facts which the sentence depicts'), and his adoption (in *Philosophical Investigations*) of a contextual view of language according to which the hypothesis of a single norm of 'objective' language is replaced by a conception of a range of discontinuous contextually determined norms of language ('language-games'). Casey's general thesis points towards the possibility of criticism as a discipline:

> One of the main effects . . . of the *Philosophical Investigations* is to destroy the idea (or prejudice) that aesthetic reasoning is essentially unlike other forms of reasoning, or that it is not genuinely rational at all. (Casey, p. 31)

The 'picture theory' is an ancient and respectable theory; its compelling power and its 'common-sense' appeal derive ultimately from the successful Baconian movement in the seventeenth century, which was reinforced by an ascendant classicism (between Cowley and Dryden). Despite the Augustans' characteristic insistence upon generality and typicality, Bacon's assumption that 'words are but the images of matter' lay beneath the often Platonic veneer of eighteenth-century poetics. The Romantics rescued poetry from the tutelage of matter and mere understanding, but failed (with the exception of Blake) to loosen the hold of the picture-view of language which left science in possession of the 'facts', left poetry the option of various forms of transcendence, and left the critic an exclusively subjective and evaluative role. What is missing is a conception of contextual norms of objectivity. Not only is Wittgenstein important here, but also R. G. Collingwood, who, in his peculiarly lucid way, refuted the Oxford 'realists' on the question of the truth and falsity of linguistic statements. His attack on propositional logic has direct relevance to the problem of 'objectivity'. The logical atomists' conception of an ideal language in which each indicative sentence expresses a unit of thought in the form of a proposition is overthrown in favour of a 'logic of question and answer':

> What is ordinarily meant when a proposition is called 'true', I thought, was this: (a) the proposition belongs to a question-

and-answer complex which as a whole is 'true' in the proper
sense of the word; (b) within this complex it is an answer to a
certain question; (c) the question is what we ordinarily call a
sensible or intelligent question, not a silly one, or in my
terminology, it 'arises'; (d) the proposition is the 'right' answer
to that question. (Collingwood, p. 38)

On this argument, a critic's theories may be seen as attempts to give
the 'right' answer to questions which 'arise' in particular question-
and-answer complexes. His answers will be 'true' (objective) if they
have an explanatory power in particular contexts. Collingwood's
defence of an independent historical methodology against the
realists' scientism has implications also for criticism as a form of
knowledge:

My 'realist' friends said . . . that their theory of knowledge was
a theory of knowledge, not a theory of this kind of knowledge
or that kind of knowledge; that certainly it applied to scientific
knowledge, but equally to historical knowledge or any other
kind I liked to name; and that it was foolish to think that one
kind of knowledge could need a special epistemological study
all to itself. I could see that they were mistaken; that in point of
fact the thing they called theory of knowledge had been
devised with special reference to the methodology of natural
science. (p. 85)

Critics have rarely crossed the fact–value divide in order to assert
the scientific status of criticism. Northrop Frye made an exhilarating
attempt to set criticism on an objective course as a discipline which
derives 'axioms' and 'postulates' from the empirical study of its
object. The conception of an independent discipline is developed by
analogy with the natural sciences, and at this general level the
analogy is a valuable polemical instrument for banishing an un-
systematic amateurish approach to criticism. However, the analogy
has damaging effects on Frye's approach to the thorny problem of
values. The 'methodology of natural science' imposes itself silently
at the centre of Frye's 'discipline'. For Frye, criticism 'is not directly
concerned with value-judgments', which are regarded either as the
manifestation of socio-ethical prejudices ('rhetorical value-judgments') or as direct personal response ('positive value-judgments'):

Thus, though the normal development of a critic's taste is towards tolerance and catholicity, still criticism as knowledge is one thing, and value-judgments informed by taste are another. The attempt to bring the direct experience of literature into the structure of criticism produces the aberrations of the history of taste already dealt with. The attempt to reverse the procedure and bring criticism into direct experience will destroy the integrity of both. Direct experience tries to be a new and fresh experience each time, which is clearly impossible if the poem itself has been replaced by a critical view of the poem. (Frye, p. 28)

The attraction of a clear-cut distinction between an objective criticism and a subjective 'experience of literature' is evident: the criteria of scientific objectivity are more nearly satisfied as the subjective experience is phased out of the critical procedure. Once again a scientific analogy is invoked:

The original experience is like the direct vision of colour or the direct sensation of heat or cold, that physics 'explains' in what, from the point of view of experience itself, is a quite irrelevant way. (p. 27)

Several objections must be made to the implications of the analogy: (1) The 'original experience' of cold bears a different relationship to physics from the relationship between criticism and the 'original experience' of a poem. Experience of a poem can hardly be limited to the kind of mere sensory stimulus involved in the experience of cold. In criticism it is hard to distinguish between 'practical criticism' and 'the original experience' of a poem; at any rate, they are necessary stages in a continuum. The experience of cold is not necessary in this sense. (2) Frye overlooks the degree to which value judgements are implicit in the criticism of literature. Pope is not preferred to Samuel Cobb for randomly historical or arbitrarily subjective reasons. The 'individual talent' of Pope outweighs that of Cobb, because the 'new (the really new) work of art' modifies the existing order of tradition. The critic, in pointing to Pope's innovative moves, has implied a value judgement in a way which is not open to the physicist whose objects are not human artefacts. (3) The relation between subject and object within the methodology of a particular discipline may vary according to the kind of questions the discipline seeks to answer. The methodology of the natural sciences, whatever that is, does not necessarily provide a universal model.

After Leavis, there was no decisive paradigm shift in English criticism. The 1950s saw the final stage in the assimilation (under the banner of Cox and Dyson) of American New Criticism, which remains for many the frontier of criticism. Its objective stance and 'intrinsic' approach to texts masked a deep commitment to an affective humanism closely affiliated to Romantic thought and implicated in a conservative ideology which preserved the Romantic notion of poetry's wholeness and concreteness as against the analytic and abstracting power of science and capitalist mass society. Its critical terms (tension, irony, indirection, complexity, ambiguity) were hived off as aesthetic concepts from an essentially humanistic discourse. The effect was to reify texts as autotelic entities, possessing their own principles of order and unity, secure from 'extrinsic' interference. Romantic 'concreteness' is preserved in the notion of a pure 'practical' criticism in which the text's immediacy makes theoretical practice redundant.

The Romantic preoccupation with the opposition between poetry and science is sustained in the New Criticism, especially in the writings of T. E. Hulme (an important precursor), John Crow Ransom and Allen Tate. William J. Handy, writing of Kant's distrust of mere logical reasoning, argued that 'This particular form of anti-intellectualism..., so important to the poetic theory of Wordsworth, Coleridge, and the romantic poets generally, is basically the same form present in the repudiation of science characteristic of present-day criticism' (p. 13). Significantly, the Kantian strain in New Criticism was not present in the Leavisian criticism in England: rather than an assertion of poetry's cognitive independence of science, we had an appeal to 'felt experience'.

In the 1960s there were no signs in England of a break with the fact–value paradigm. The stylistics of Ullman and Spitzer, and the historical poetics of Auerbach and Curtius were little known. But since the late 1960s, there has been a flood of translations of European philosophy, semiotics, structuralism, psychoanalysis, Marxism and other social theory, begun in the Marxist Journal *New Left Review*, and sustained in *Screen*, *Twentieth-Century Studies*, *Oxford Literary Review* and a number of other influential post-structuralist, Marxist or feminist publications. The alien presences stimulated a decade of tireless assimilation, restless improvisation and generally a bewildering flux of approaches, none of which assumed a clear predominance. A substantial avant-garde of Marxist, feminist, structuralist and post-structuralist groups and tendencies has evolved. The hegemony exercised by the older Leavisian, New Critical and traditional practices has been challenged but not displaced. For the first time in English criticism 'theory' has been placed on the agenda. But before we have had time to speak about theory, the disciples of Derrida threaten to remove it in favour of a 'deconstructive' practice which subverts its own status as theoretical discourse.

The extent and the limits of the revolution in English criticism are reflected in the changes in the writings of David Lodge, a critic who has remained faithfully English in his scepticism, empiricism and common sense, and yet who has been moved to abandon silently earlier positions. In *Language of Fiction* (1966) he introduced to English novel criticism the methods of Wayne Booth, Wimsatt, Mark Schorer and others. However, his remarks on linguistics revealed his strong attachment to the distinction between 'emotive' and 'referential' language uses. Linguistics, he argues, will never replace or challenge literary criticism,[1] because 'It is the essential characteristic of modern linguistics that it claims to be a science. It is the essential characteristic of literature that it concerns values. And values are not amenable to scientific method' (p. 57). His later writings, notably *Modes of Modern Writing* (1977), retain a strong (and admirable) emphasis on practical criticism, but the fact–value dischotomy is no longer present to obstruct the assimilation of linguistic theory to critical practice. Lodge would argue that linguistics has not displaced criticism, but has been found useful as a critical tool. However, in *Modes*, Jakobson's theory about metaphor and metonymy, evolved from Saussurian linguistics, provides the conceptual frame for the entire book. With the entry of 'theory', the fact–value distinction disappears. Lodge's rigour reduces Jakobson's concepts to empirical generalisations, which are dissolved and rendered harmless in a rich profusion of actual texts. In so far as the persistence of empiricism in English criticism has been the securer and preserver of the fact–value dichotomy, the advance of 'theory' is bound to be illusory, until a real 'break' with empiricism's hegemony occurs.

Note

1 One might compare the debate between F. W. Bateson and Roger Fowler (*Essays in Criticism*) in 1967. Bateson adopted the fact-value distinction in his attacks on linguistics claims to critical authority. Not surprisingly he considered Wordsworth 'not primarily a thinker but a feeler' (Bateson, pp. 39-40). See also Hayes.

3

Literary Criticism and Science

Academics are usually quick to defend the interests and dignity of their disciplines, but are not always able to justify the attribution of the title 'discipline' to their often time-honoured and respected activities. While scientists are normally able to give an account of the bases of their disciplines (at least provisionally), the social scientist and particularly the historian and literary critic are less successful. The social sciences are a battleground for contending accounts of their disciplines: the battle-lines are drawn up between the various contenders for the throne, but the issue is very much in doubt. In England literary critics, for the most part, have been sublimely unaware of or uninterested in the problem. Historically, one might regard this state of affairs as a reflection of the uneven development of the various fields. The situation in sociology, for example, might be said to resemble the condition of the natural sciences in the seventeenth century, while the situation in criticism is more like the state of the natural sciences in the pre-Socratic period. On this view, one might look forward to the ultimate emergence of a 'science' of sociology, and perhaps, in the dim and distant future, a 'science' of criticism. One can imagine the critic, emerging momentarily from his or her enraptured perusal of a Shakespeare sonnet, declaring: 'Surely not a *science* of criticism?' They need not fear the worst: I would not suggest for one moment that he should be robbed of his ecstasy and that she be flung headlong into a cold bath of empiricism. Both 'science' and 'discipline' are guilty words, deeply stained in our culture's sins of omission. We cannot hope to render the words innocent by the sheer force of argument, but, if we handle them gingerly, we may be able to teach them new habits.

What is a Discipline?

How might one provisionally describe a discipline? At least two aspects of intellectual activity suggest themselves: a practical and a theoretical. On the one hand a discipline is a body of *practices* (methods and procedures of analysis and study) which constitutes a skill. On the other hand, it is a body of *concepts*, forming a framework for the production of knowledge. Certain 'subjects' claiming the status of disciplines (language teaching, professional training) have a primarily practical character. Other 'subjects' have a primarily or purely conceptual character. But in those 'subjects' whose concern is with the production of knowledge the two aspects are both present and in constant interaction. The problems about the nature of disciplines which affect literary criticism are problems which affect not so much the purely 'practical' subjects nor the purely conceptual subjects, but those disciplines which involve a crucial interplay between theory and practice. I prefer to regard mathematics and philosophy as metadisciplines whose main significance lies in their relationships with other disciplines.

Tentatively, then, let us define a discipline as a developing body of concepts whose efficacy in the production of knowledge is determined by acceptable procedures of validation. The acceptability of the procedures, in my view, is determined by the internal requirements of the discipline and by the nature of its object. The criteria of objectivity in a discipline are ultimately matters of consensus among the members of a discipline. In the natural sciences the predominance of a 'value-free', 'neutral' language of communication and observation is the result of *choice*: such a mode of discourse has proved more effective in the domain of the natural world. The convention of 'non-involvement' has not proved particularly effective in the other disciplines. This argument is based upon the assumption that disciplines are not definable in terms of some universal logic of scientific discovery or of any other monistic conception of knowledge (whether empiricist or idealist), but rather on the grounds of some kind of internal coherence. Such a view will inevitably invite scepticism: 'If a discipline can define its own criteria of validation, then a group of religious fanatics would have as much claim to be the practitioners of a discipline as a group of physicists.' It must be replied that to reject a monistic view is not to embrace a total relativism and scepticism. 'Coherence' would certainly require a commitment not merely to consensus but also to the values of rationality and empirical evidence. One is faced here with the need to question the dichotomy between 'science' and 'non-science', a distinction which has played a large part in creating the problems with which this book is concerned.

The Distinction between Scientific and Non-Scientific

The notion that literature is a form of experience or of language which possesses a high degree of non-rational content has a long history. Plato's Ion argued that the gods take away the poets' senses in order to inspire them with divine frenzy: 'No man can compose or prophesy so long as he has his reason' (Russell and Winterbottom, p. 43). Longinus too stressed the importance of emotion in sublime poetry. In the Romantic period the dichotomy between poetry and science developed on the basis of an identification of poetry and feeling. We have seen that, since the Romantics, the distinction between emotive and referential uses of language has been sustained almost until the present. The logical positivists' arguments clearly implied not only that poetic language does not make statements about the world but also that the evaluative language of criticism itself has no status as knowledge.

To call literature non-scientific is one thing, but to call criticism non-scientific is another. Critics themselves have tended to elide the two statements. Most agree that the important literary texts do not give us a conceptual knowledge of the world, but an affective or intuitive experience of it. F. R. Leavis argued that poetry does not deal in analysable statements but in the enactment and realisation of experience in non-reducible poetic terms. He goes on, in his debate with René Wellek in the 1930s, to claim that *criticism* also is concerned with 'feeling into' and not with 'thinking about' literature. On this view, criticism has no theoretical dimension and no objective status. Leavis's position seems to be that criticism *points out* the modes of poetic enactment of experience as they are embodied in the best works of literature, but does not construct a *knowledge* of literature in conceptual terms. The philosopher, he suggests, may be interested in constructing such a knowledge, but it is not the critic's province. I would argue that a knowledge of literature can be constructed only from within criticism itself on the basis of the 'practical' work of critics (Selden, 1975).

A major obstacle to the recognition of the cognitive claims of the social and human sciences has been the philosophers' desire to establish a demarcation principle which will unequivocally distinguish science from non-science. The logical positivists argued that knowledge of the world may be constructed only from propositions based upon sense experience. If a sentence does not 'refer' to sense experience then it is unscientific: if no possible observation is relevant to its truth value, it is not a scientific statement. But their principle of 'verification' did not stand up to much inspection, because it became clear that no finite number of observations could ever verify a universal statement. Einstein had displaced Newtonian mechanics, which had been a well-attested theory. There could be no guarantee that Einstein's theory would not also be displaced. As is well known, Popper seemed to have solved this difficulty by proposing a principle of 'falsification', according to which a theory is scientific in so far as it is open to refutation. On this model, the progress of science consists in the gradual whittling down of the number of competing theories. Theories which do not permit refutation are non-scientific and 'metaphysical' (for example those of Freud and Marx). Imre Lakatos pointed out that the most serious weakness in Popper's position was his failure to establish why specific anomalies should be regarded as refutations in some contexts and only as 'exceptions' in others (see Lakatos and Musgrave, pp. 91–196). There seem to be no clear grounds for distinguishing between a theory heading for refutation as a result of anomalies and a theory progressing in an upward trend despite anomalies. A more general criticism which might be made of Popper's position is that its orientation is negative – towards problems of refutation and error, rather than towards problems of theory-production.

The work of T. S. Kuhn and P. Feyerabend has drawn attention to the radical discontinuities in the history of science. Kuhn argued that 'normal science' involves the acceptance of fundamental conceptual premises which he calls 'paradigms'. The paradigm determines the questions asked and the experiments set up; most scientists are engaged in the articulation and full exploration of the implications of a particular paradigm. Paradigms are accepted despite awareness of anomalies, but the presence of anomalies may also provide the motivation for a major paradigm revision. The example of the discovery of oxygen is instructive. Lavoisier was aware that something was wrong with the phlogiston theory of combustion long before he became involved in the discovery of oxygen. Joseph Priestley, working happily with the phlogiston concept, failed to see the presence of oxygen in a sample successfully produced in the course of wider experiments on 'air' emitted by solid bodies. He thought it was dephlogisticated air. Lavoisier, already convinced that burning bodies absorbed some part of the atmosphere, was able to recognise the significance of Priestley's experiments.

The implications of this example are far-reaching. Conceptual adjustments (or paradigm revision) may be responsible for the perception of 'facts'. The phlogiston theory did not permit the construction of the fact of oxygen. 'Oxygen' as a 'fact' is constituted by the new theory of combustion. Feyerabend states the principle clearly:

> Not only is the description of every single fact dependent on *some* theory (which may, of course, be very different from the theory to be tested). There exist also facts which cannot be unearthed except with the help of alternatives to the theory to be tested, and which become unavailable as soon as such alternatives are excluded. (Feyerabend, 1968, p. 27)

What are the implications of these developments in the philosophy of science for critical theory? First, some of the objections to a theoretical role for criticism have less force, in view of the fact that observation and experiment seem to be less crucial to the development of the natural sciences than was once thought. The new emphasis on the generative importance of *conceptual* shifts has the effect of making the social sciences and the human sciences appear less non-scientific. Or, one might say, the sciences now appear less 'scientific'. The 'facts' of literary criticism, like those of sociology, and of quantum mechanics, are crucially constituted by the paradigms currently in force. Principles of empirical evidence are still required, but the criteria of acceptability of evidence can no longer be dogmatically enunciated. In the absence of a bold and naked confrontation with the realm of 'facts', we are left with a notion of disciplines as changing frameworks of concepts whose explanatory power depends less upon a *logic* of discovery than upon the acceptance of the frameworks as working models by the members of the disciplines. New paradigms throw up new problems for 'normal' science to solve, but they have no absolute status as *laws*. On the other hand, as I shall argue later, we are not compelled to assume that all paradigm shifts are merely random reorientations of conceptual systems. Knowledge may always be provisional and 'incomplete', but it may still be more or less effective in giving us the 'real'.

Two other problems which are intimately connected with the demarcation issue are (1) the problem of the fact–value dichotomy and (2) the problem of the relation between subject and object in the realm of knowledge. The demarcation lines between science and non-science are often enforced by the fact–value distinction. Science operates in the domain of 'facts', while criticism operates in the realm of 'values'. Critics normally accept this line of demarcation, sometimes wholeheartedly in the name of intuition and anti-intellectual humanism, or reluctantly in the name of objectivity. Norman Rodway accepted that criticism is essentially a subjective and value-laden activity, but claimed that it can be partially re-deemed if the critic develops a 'grasp of logic' and 'habit of detach-ment' which will help him or her to temper the subjectivity of opinion (Rodway, p. 224). One senses here the uneasiness we found earlier in J. S. Mill. The experience of the social sciences has demonstrated the cognitive impoverishment which results when writers adopt uncritically the norms of objectivity supposed to be operative in the natural sciences. Some remarks by Norbert Elias are pertinent here:

Hence the use, in social sciences, of a method akin to that evolved in the physical sciences often gives to the former the appearance of a high level of detachment or of 'objectivity' which those who use this method are in fact lacking. It often serves as a means of circumventing difficulties which spring from their dilemma without facing it; in many cases, it creates a facade of detachment masking a highly involved approach. (Elias, p. 240)

The demarcation issue also raises the difficult problem of the relation between subject and object in the domain of knowledge. I have already suggested that the philosophy of science has begun to question the empiricist epistemology which conceives of knowledge as a series of universal or general statements abstracted from the observation of facts: the empiricist model of knowledge is identified with the model of sense perception, especially vision. Without adopting a Kantian scepticism ('We cannot know "things in themselves"'), it can be argued that knowledge is more like a mode of production than a mirror reflection. Roy Bhaskar's generalisation about scientific theories makes this assumption: 'In real history scientific theories do not spring from the void – but from the development and reworking of cognitive material that pre-exists them, necessitating the creative employment of ideas from adjacent fields' (Bhaskar, p. 37). The use of analogies and models in the natural sciences suggests a much more *poetic* theory of scientific knowledge, and draws attention to the similarities between 'scientific' and 'non-scientific' disciplines, rather than the differences. William James's account of scientific 'genius' is strikingly poetic in conception:

> The flash of similarity between an apple and the moon, between the rivalry for food in nature and the rivalry for man's selection, was too recondite for any but the exceptional minds. Genius, then . . . is identical with the possession of similar association to an extreme degree. (cit. Leatherdale, p. 14)

Many staunch advocates of an empiricist method in science have no difficulty in accepting that major theories involve imaginative leaps, but insist that the leaps are always safely reabsorbed into the conventional modes of rationality and subjected to universally acknowledged objective controls. They easily forget that the major advances in physics during this century have involved an increasing degree of idealisation and abstraction; the articulation of theories by means of logico-mathematical models *disconnects* the theory from an empirical 'reality' which it seeks to understand (see Winterbourne, p. 259; Macherey, 1978, pp. 5–7).

The Problem of Objectivity

The lessons literary critics can learn from Kuhn are various and conflicting. His fellow philosophers of science have attacked him on several grounds, but a key objection centres on the problem of objectivity. Kuhn himself has complained that a misleading subjective–objective dichotomy has been forced upon him. He acknowledged that his work has drawn attention to the element of *choice* and *judgement* involved in theory evaluation: there is no universal criterion of correct theory choice, no single algorithm one can apply regardless of personal and historical context. All scientific communities, he agrees, possess criteria according to which they evaluate new theories. Kuhn suggests five criteria: accuracy, consistency, breadth of scope, simplicity and fruitfulness. He goes on to warn that not only will people apply the criteria differently, but also the criteria will often provide conflicting values (one theory may be simple, inaccurate and fruitful; another accurate, complex and unfruitful). Kuhn draws attention to the extent to which major scientific theories have conflicted with particular criteria. The competition between Ptolemaic and Copernican astronomy was in many ways weighted in favour of the older theory: heliocentric astronomy was inconsistent with other scientific theories (which depended upon geocentricity); Copernicus's theory could not even claim greater accuracy, until Kepler's revisions allowed this criterion to be applied.

The criteria which guide choice 'function not as rules, which determine choice, but as values, which influence it' (Kuhn, 1977, p. 331). Kuhn is surely right in suggesting that a change in values often triggers a change in theory choice. Bacon's philosophy established a new matrix of values which profoundly influenced modern physical science: utility became an important criterion and absorbed the concept of fruitfulness for a time. The application and weighting of values have varied historically in ways which have influenced scientific theories. Accuracy of a numerical kind was not stressed in early modern science except in astronomy and was only later applied to chemistry and other disciplines. It is also important to Kuhn's arguments that scientists themselves are the bearers of values: he believes that their personal histories and experience will affect their choices and application of criteria. Kuhn, it seems, vacillates between an individual (psychological) and a collective (sociological) explanation. His theory of paradigms excludes a purely individual account of scientific 'advance' and yet his essay on 'theory choice' places a greater stress on personal factors. Even when he is discussing the commitments of the scientific community he puts his arguments in subjective terms: 'scientists who share the concerns and sensibilities of the individual who discovers a new theory are ipso facto likely to appear disproportionately frequently among that theory's first supporters' (Kuhn, 1977, p. 328). Kuhn defends himself against those critics who believe that his position makes theory choice undiscussible, 'a matter of taste'; his view is 'subjective' only in the sense that he considers theory choice to be *judgemental* and not the automatic product of a universal set of criteria.

Kuhn's intervention questioned the dominant empiricist 'ideology' of science. Israel Scheffler's reply reasserts the 'ideal of objectivity' which rests upon observational control. Scheffler argues that while observation is not free of conceptualisation, the observed entities are not predetermined by the category systems adopted by the observer. Categories, he argues, are simply pigeon-holes for the sorting of items, and might be sharply distinguished from hypotheses which make truth claims by predicting the assignment of items. Conflicting hypotheses may be understood under the rubric 'different assignment under the selfsame category system' (Scheffler, p. 39). He rejects Kuhn's concept of the non-translatable nature of hypotheses. While Scheffler insists on the irreducible objectivity of 'items', Kuhn believes that 'facts' cannot be separated from the category systems favoured by particular scientific communities. The application of category systems in literary criticism tends to support Kuhn's contention. The conflict between Aristotle's and Coleridge's categories does not allow an appeal to literary 'items' as ultimate observed entities, except in the minimal sense of 'texts'. The categories 'fancy' and 'imagination' predetermine to a large extent the observed distinctions between texts: Cowley is 'fanciful', Milton 'imaginative'. I. A. Richards's revaluation of Coleridge's categories appears to confirm Scheffler's claim that conflicting theories may be understood as involving 'different assignment under the selfsame category system'. However, Richards is using an anti-Romantic neo-positivist set of assumptions to undermine Coleridge's idealist hierarchies (organic/mechanical, imaginative/fanciful). Between

Coleridge and Richards a 'paradigm shift' had occurred; Coleridge's categories had undergone a sea change and become part of a new critical matrix, capable of producing quite different readings of texts. If one accepts that T. E. Hulme and I. A. Richards laid the foundations of a new critical paradigm, the decline in Milton's standing during the early period of New Criticism and the elevation of metaphysical poetry can be understood as the effect of reworking Romantic categories into a quite different pattern of concepts.

If we assume the possibility of an 'objective knowledge' of literary production, must we assess and compare the validity of Coleridge's and Richards's critical systems? Should we assume some kind of historical progression from the mystified to the demystified? Should we regard their respective systems as historically conditioned and therefore incommensurable? Can we employ the methods and criteria of the natural sciences as a means of assessing critical validity? These are some of the questions raised by our reflections on the philosophy of science. William Blake's dialectic of Reason and Energy provides a model which makes some sense of the 'progression' of knowledge. Scientific revolutions often involve the denial of an existing rational consensus.

While Scheffler, and before him Lakatos and Popper, would not have denied the role of imagination in scientific discovery, they part company with Kuhn and Feyerabend on the question of objective controls. For Scheffler, objectivity resides in the process of justification, not invention or creativity: 'Underlying historical changes of theory, there is ... a continuity of logic and method, which unifies each scientific age with that which preceded it' (p. 9). Feyerabend's 'anarchist' philosophy of science argues that there is a basic *antagonism* between the tenets of scientific rationalism and the development of science:

> The principles of critical rationalism ... and of logical empiricism ... give an inadequate account of science because science is much more 'sloppy' and 'irrational' than its methodological image.... For what appears as 'sloppiness', 'chaos' or 'opportunism' when compared with [the 'laws of reason'] has a most important function in the development of ... theories.... *These 'deviations', these 'errors', are preconditions of progress*...without 'chaos', no knowledge. Without

frequent dismissal of reason, no progress. (Feyerabend, 1977)

Feyerabend here gives us a Blakean view of reason as a deadening force of *conformity* and *convention* in normal science. One must add that, after a major break, the newly irrupted theory requires its followers to uphold it with the rigour and commitment of a convert, thus imposing a new rationality. Polyani's comment on the positive power of a normative rationality balances Feyerabend's anarchism: 'a theory which we acclaim as rational in itself is thereby accredited with prophetic powers' (p. 5).

Polyani's account of Einstein's Special Theory of Relativity is especially interesting. It is usually thought that the Michelson–Morley experiment in 1887 provided the basic empirical evidence upon which Einstein's theory was built. However, Polyani points out that Einstein's 1905 paper was not a response to the earlier experiment but an independently intuited theory, influenced rather by the positivist Mach than by any immediately empirical demand. Further, D. C. Miller's experiments between 1902 and 1926 provided empirical evidence that the Michelson–Morley findings should be revised and that there was after all a 'positive effect' (that is, the speed of light *had* been affected by the earth's movement in the ether). Far from dropping Einstein's theory, by that time (1925) scientists 'had so closed their minds to any suggestion which threatened the new rationality achieved by Einstein's world-picture, that it was almost impossible for them to think again in different terms' (p. 13). It was only later that experiments were set up which provided more accurate measurements in support of the original Michelson–Morley results. Some elements in this narrative support an objectivity of universal criteria (the accurate measurements provided the ultimate imprimatur); others support a more 'creative' notion of objectivity. It seems reasonable to suggest that the dilemma is created by the objective–subjective dualism itself, and that we should explore the problem in terms of alternative concepts of objectivity rather than in terms of a rigid polarity, even though I realise that I appear to be in danger of making redundant the whole notion of objective knowledge. It has often been pointed out that in other cultures the concept of knowledge has not been riven by dualism as it has been in Britain, but, as we saw in the last chapter, the repercussions of this dualism on British criticism have been far-reaching. To redefine the concept of knowledge in terms of an enlarged objectivity is a form of intervention, in a historically protracted debate, which does not entail conceding the territory of knowledge to the scientific positivist.

Kuhn's theories have the effect of closing the gap between the natural sciences and the human 'sciences'. The scientism of certain critical formalisms has never become the dominant mode, and Kuhn's work supports the view that literary criticism would be wrong to look for objective standards and methods in the positivist and empiricist philosophies of science. At this point many literary critics will breathe a sigh of relief and turn back to their unself-conscious ways, or, like David Bleich, they may be encouraged by Kuhn's emphasis upon psychological motivations to adopt some kind of individualistic relativism. However, the concept of 'paradigm' also has strongly *collective* and *historical* implications, which allow a more 'objective' view.

The denial of linear 'progress' in the history of science appears to undermine an essential requirement of an objective position. How-ever, an objective position is what is to be defined and is not an assumed set of universal criteria to be used to define itself. Kuhn was not the first to reject a view of science as aggregation. A. N. White-head approaches a similar perspective when he writes of Descartes and William James: 'They each of them open an epoch by their clear formulation of terms in which thought could profitably express itself at particular stages of knowledge.' (p. 205) This perspective potentially includes the notion of 'breaks' and at the same time pre-serves 'stages'. It allows no linear 'progress' but conceives knowledge as a series of conceptual clusters, advancing by breaks and jumps rather than by incremental or evolutionary phases. Science does not progress by a steady refinement and a purer apprehension of a pre-existent world of objective 'facts'. One must add that within 'knowledge' there are regions and subregions which advance in an uneven way. Within particular regions, the transitions do not signify simply a cancellation or annulment of earlier phases. Paradigms are 'worked' and exhausted; old paradigms remain as revered marks of achieved knowledge.

If we say that the history of a region of knowledge does not advance along an upward path of progress, have we also excluded the notion of a transition from non-scientific or pre-scientific stages to science as such? Levi-Strauss's 'Science of the Concrete' (*The Savage Mind*, 1966) regards the 'knowledge' of primitive societies as 'scientific' in its reduction of the objective universe to conceptual categories: such mapping and ordering of experience involve a different application of criteria of rationality, but the knowledge possesses the same function in society of making sense of the material world. By applying Kuhn's criteria of scientific value to the extreme case of primitive knowledge, we highlight a crucial question: do paradigm shifts ever involve a passage from pre-scientific to scientific, or from common sense to science, or from ideology to science?

This question has been debated with the deepest insight in the Marxist tradition, especially since Louis Althusser's *For Marx* was published in English in 1969. The French philosopher argued that the writings of Marx should be divided between an 'ideological' period before, and a 'scientific' period after the 'epistemological break' which occurred in 1845. The emergence of a science involves a break from a whole frame of reference of pre-scientific (ideological) notions and the construction of a new pattern, or 'problematic'. With Marx, argues Althusser, a break from Hegelian and Feuerbachian problematics announces the emergence of a science of history involving the articulation of the basic concepts of dialectical and historical materialism. This whole approach has not been well received in Britain. Many English Marxists, notably Raymond Williams and E. P. Thompson, have stoutly defended the humanist Marx, especially associated with the *1844 Manuscripts*, which Althusser called 'that genial synthesis of Feuerbach and Hegel' (*For Marx*, p. 36). Any notion of Marx's *scientific* revolution has the ring of formalism and theoreticism to an English ear brought up on the tones of F. R. Leavis or William Morris. This tradition cannot conceive of an objective knowledge, in whatever region of knowledge, which is not governed by the individual's experience within a particular social order. The only thing which prevents the humanist approach from plunging into a Kuhnian relativism is the concept of class struggle: knowledge arises as the effect of the historian's or critic's commitment to the perspective and struggle of the oppressed and submerged working people. Such knowledge is inseparable from a humanistic stance; a set of values and a vision of a free and full humanity, which will supersede bourgeois humanism, is the very site of a true knowledge for the Marxist humanist. Louis Althusser's 'theoretical anti-humanism' has been much misunderstood by English Marxists. It has nothing to do with practical politics: Althusser recognises the need for a socialist humanism to replace the dominant bourgeois images of the human. He argues that an 'anti-humanism' in the domain of *theory* is essential if we are to understand Marx's fundamental break from a Feuerbachian preoccupation with 'Man' as the central category of historical explanation; we must question

> the *theoretical* pretensions of the humanist conception to explain society and history, starting out from the human essence, from the free human subject, the subject of needs, of labour, of desire, the subject of moral and political action. I maintain that Marx was only able to found the science of history and to write *Capital* because he broke with the *theoretical* pretensions of all such varieties of humanism. (Althusser, 1976, p. 201)

This anti-humanism is, then, essential, if we are to mark in thought the transition from an ideological to a scientific knowledge.

The Althusser of *For Marx* conceives ideology as 'the *lived* relationship between men and their world' (p. 233); it appears as 'conscious', but this consciousness is only of an 'imaginary' relationship to the real world, masking an 'unconscious' *real* relationship:

> Thus, in a very exact sense, the bourgeoisie *lives* in the ideology of *freedom* the relation between it and its conditions of existence: that is, *its* real relation (the law of a liberal capitalist economy) *but invested in an imaginary relation* (all men are free, including the free labourers). (p. 234)

Althusser admits that ideology is a structure essential to the historical existence of all societies, and that therefore we cannot envisage a passage beyond ideology or a society which can do without it. He is careful to emphasise that ideology is not merely a matter of a people's consciousness, but is 'lived' as 'an object of their "world" – as their "world" itself'. Individuals, he argued later in *Lenin and Philosophy*, are constituted as 'subjects' by ideology which 'hails' or 'interpellates' them: the hailing is done through an Ideological State

Apparatus (ISA), which may be educational, religious, familial, political, 'cultural' or communicational. ISAs all contribute to the reproduction of the existing relations of production. Althusser considered the School to be the dominant apparatus in modern society, and his disciple Pierre Macherey has based much of his work on this emphasis. Althusser's theory of ISAs has been criticised from several angles. From a Lacanian perspective, the Althusserian 'subject' is no more than the bearer of a structure which is already in place; the psychoanalytic 'subject' is necessarily eccentric and disruptive (MacCabe, 1981, pp. 210–17). From a Marxist viewpoint, the concept of 'ideology in general' does not permit a proper understanding of ideological struggle (Laclau, pp. 92–111). Despite these criticisms the concept 'interpellation' retains great theoretical value, as Laclau has shown (see Chapter 4).

Unlike a dominant ideology, which when smoothly functioning transforms individuals into subjects fitted to their places in the historical set of economic and social relations into which they are born, knowledge does not depend on the category of the subject, but is the product of theoretical practice: the work of transforming ideological concepts into knowledge is a process without a subject. On this point Kuhn's concept of paradigms or Foucault's *episteme* help us to understand Althusser. Scientific revolutions are not 'discoveries' of 'facts' made by individual scientists in the privacy of their laboratories. Rather, revolutions are 'moments' when a conceptual rupture allows a new domain of the 'real' to emerge, and to be worked over by researchers who share the new conceptual pattern. Marx, reworking the already existing but 'ideological' concepts of Feuerbach and others at a particular historical conjuncture, initiated a new knowledge, a knowledge of history.

The transition from an ideological to a scientific stage is hard to theorise, if we adopt Althusser's highly abstract category of 'ideology in general'. Georges Canguilhem developed the concept of 'scientific ideology' in order to clarify the history of the sciences. He makes an important distinction between a scientific ideology and a superstition or false belief:

> within scientific ideology there exists the explicit intention of being a science, of imitating some model of an already existing science. . . . The existence of scientific ideologies implies that

parallel scientific discourses already exist and . . . that the
separation of science and religion has already been enacted.
(Canguilhem, p. 22)

This helps us to make a more refined distinction between scientific
and ideological discourses. For example, Herbert Spencer's system
of general evolution draws upon established scientific discourses,
especially Darwin's biology, in order to establish a scientific
ideology, whose function was to legitimise free enterprise and its
ideological supports (individualism and competition). Modern
ethology, linguistics and sociology have established Spencer's
ideological status, while Darwin remains as a founding father of a
science:

> an ideology disappears when the conditions that make it a
> historical possibility have also disappeared. The scientific
> theory of evolution has not remained exactly what Darwinism
> was; for Darwinism is only a moment integral to the history of
> the constitution of the science of evolution. By contrast,
> evolutionist ideology has remained a sterile residue within the
> history of 19th-century social science. (ibid., p. 24)

The distinction between a scientific ideology and a science is
evidently required if one considers the notorious 'Lysenko affair' of
1948. The emerging (Mendelian) science of genetics was outlawed in
the USSR, dismissed as 'bourgeois science' and replaced by a true
'proletarian science', the half-baked theories of Lysenko. The official
state version of dialectical materialism (essentially Engels's *Anti-
Dühring* as epitomised by Stalin) was used to install Lysenkoism as
the only science of heredity faithful to Marxism-Leninism (see
Lecourt). It should be made clear that the attack on genetics was not
merely an assertion of the class nature of genetics as an institutional
practice, but as a set of concepts and theories.

Canguilhem's theory helps us deal with certain other awkward
questions. What prevents an epistemological break occurring in the
future which will make a region of knowledge appear as mere
ideology or at most pre-scientific? Is it perhaps the universal effect of
new knowledge to give old knowledges the appearance of being
ideologies or myths? It is only recently that the application to
Renaissance alchemy of the distinction between pre-scientific and

scientific has been seriously questioned. A theory of historical discontinuities keeps coming up against powerful arguments for continuities. In his *Essays in Self-Criticism* Althusser confesses that, by conceiving the transition from ideology to science as a *theoretical* break, he made a 'theoreticist' error. He acknowledges that the theoretical break made by Marx cannot be separated from the break he made with bourgeois ideology in support of a proletarian ideology. The new knowledge cannot be divorced from the historical conjuncture in which it occurred. This knowledge is not once and for all, because the labour of producing and reproducing knowledge can never cease: 'only the production of new knowledge keeps old knowledge alive'. Without new knowledge the old knowledge becomes a dogma, dead and ossified. Marxism then runs the risk of 'repeating truths which are no longer any more than the names of things, when the world is demanding new knowledge' in response to a changing historical reality: 'Marxist theory can fall behind history, and even behind itself, if ever it believes that it has arrived' (p. 195). Althusser is not adopting a Kuhnian relativism but a dialectical view of the production of knowledge: the old knowledge is preserved in its supervention. This dialectical development within knowledge is inseparable from the political and ideological struggles which arise in specific historical situations. Thus, Perry Anderson's brief but masterly *Considerations on Western Marxism* (1976) traces the developments in Marxist theory since Marx and Engels in terms of the relationship between theoretic work and the state of working-class struggles in specific countries at particular conjunctures. He concludes that 'the questions left unanswered by Lenin's generation, and made impossible to answer by the rupture of theory and practice in Stalin's epoch, continue to await replies.... They concern the central economic and political realities that have dominated world history in the last fifty years' (p. 103).

The gulf between Kuhn's and Althusser's position is now apparent. Scientific revolutions, in Kuhn's view, result from changes in the application of the criteria for judging scientific objectivity; the changes may arise from the personal histories of individual scientists. In Althusser's view, scientific 'breaks' are bound up with the development of class struggles: Marx's opening up of historical knowledge was inseparable from his identification with the practical struggles of the European working classes in the

1840s. To take an example of a different kind, it is evident that the development of the natural sciences in the seventeenth century in Britain was part of a larger and highly complex social transformation, which can be summed up in only the most schematic fashion. The transformation arose from the conflict between Stuart absolutist aspirations and the interests of a parliamentary alliance between large sections of the gentry and nobility together with a large, newly developed class of urban merchants, all of whom had been excluded from the monarch's distribution of monopolies and other largess. The one hundred years following the regicide saw the establishment of empire, trade and scientific activity in something like their modern forms. The practical and utilitarian ideology of Bacon's philosophy of science became the common sense of a general scientific ideology only after the defeat of the absolutist cause and the establishment of an overall ideological consensus which reflected the changed nature of social and economic relations. In these circumstances natural sciences flourished.

To argue that forms of knowledge arise and develop in relation to larger historical developments is not to accept a crude socio-economic determinism. The uneven development of forms of knowledge means that they cannot be regarded as simple non-contradictory reflections of some 'real' history.

What sort of literary theory is possible in the present historical situation remains to be seen, but there is no reason for critics to regard themselves as eternal exiles from the land of knowledge. The philosophers of science have dismantled many of the barriers which have traditionally separated 'art' and 'science'. They have also opened a historical perspective which shows us that scientific knowledge is not governed by observation and experiment but is founded upon conceptual change. The writings of Althusser and Canguilhem introduced important, though elusive, distinctions between ideological and scientific discourses. Without these, knowledge is a concept governed entirely by historical relativity, which means that criticism could be no more than an ever-so-refined expression of ideological discourse. What kind of criticism falls within our definition of conceptual knowledge? The next chapter will examine the engagement between Marxism and Russian Formalism in the 1920s, when the main subject of debate was the Formalists' claim to have founded a science of literary criticism.

4

Russian Formalism, Marxism and 'Relative Autonomy'

In 1929 Roman Jakobson remarked on the basic ambiguity of Marxist literary theorising, which oscillated uneasily between a purely genetic and a quasi-structuralist approach to literature (Erlich, p. 116 n.). This ambiguity was at least partly the result of a genuine attempt on the part of Soviet Marxists of the mid-1920s to assimilate some aspects of the Formalists' method to dialectical materialism. Attempts at synthesis were also made by the Formalists (notably Shklovsky and Eichenbaum). But, on both sides these gestures not only failed to resolve theoretical problems but also may even have contributed to the premature interruption of the encounter between Formalism and Marxism, which in the proto-structuralist work of Jakobson, Tynyanov and the Bachtin school had begun to produce results. Instead, Tynyanov turned to the writing of historical novels; Jakobson, who left Russia earlier in the 1920s, continued his structuralist studies in a different theoretical climate in Prague and later in America; Voloshinov disappeared. By 1934 (the First All-Union Congress of Soviet Writers) Formalism was totally identified with bourgeois decadence and escapism.

I would like to argue that not only did the demise of Formalism interrupt the exploration of a new theoretical domain, but also the subsequent history of structuralist poetics and its adjacent cultural theories have failed to enter the territory glimpsed by the late Formalists at a particular conjuncture. The triumph of synchrony in the work of the structuralists closed a particular form of dialogue between Formalism and Marxism which began to bear fruit in the late 1920s.

Four concepts were contested, implicitly or explicitly, in the debates between the two sides during the 1920s in Russia:

1 The concept of 'materialism', which involved the solution of

certain questions about the ontological status of art.

2 The concept of mimesis (representation), which raised questions of epistemology.

3 The concept of system and the autonomy of structures.

4 The related distinction between diachrony and synchrony, particularly as it affected relations between literary 'evolution' and socio-economic 'evolution'.

Formalism and Materialism

It is impossible to dissociate the Formalists' response to the theoretical challenges of the October Revolution from those of related groups, particularly the Futurists and the Constructivists. In many respects the Formalists' early work is dominated by their wish to theorise the practice of the Futurists' poetic work, although this was soon transformed into an attempt to establish a general 'science' of poetics.

The early polemics of the Futurists ('A Slap in the Face of Public Taste', 1912) were directed against the culture of the decadent bourgeoisie and especially against the aesthetics of symbolism. The main enemy was metaphysics. The symbolists' pseudo-mystical flirtations with the 'Absolute' and their insistence that the poet was the 'guardian of the mystery' (Erlich, p. 48) were derided by the Futurists who exulted in a new materialist rhetoric. Mayakovsky announced that poetry was a kind of production. But the reaction to symbolism was not in the direction of a realistic aesthetic, but of a radically anti-mimetic formalism. Unlike their Italian counterparts, early Russian Futurists were totally indifferent to content. They rejected the 'traditional subservience to meaning' in favour of a total commitment to 'the self-sufficient word'. In Khlebnikov's 'trans-sense' verse, there is, if not an escape from, at least an evasion of semantics; the verbal material itself (phonic and graphic) is the new 'content'. In a sense this represents a materialist inversion of the art for art's sake isolation of the aesthetic sphere. The idealist metaphysics are negated, but the autotelic status of art survives in a demystified form; as in Feuerbach's inversion of Hegel, the problematic remains unchanged (see Pike, pp. 2–4; Gray, p. 6).

After the October Revolution, the Futurists were the only important group of artists to make a firm commitment to the revolution. This gave them a leading role in the theoretical debates of the following few years. In the magazine *Art of the Commune*, the rhetoric of materialism became specifically proletarian. The artist was assimilated to the industrial artisan. The anti-mimetic drive of Futurist poetics was given a new direction. Rejecting the imitation of nature, they asserted a commitment to the role of *producer*, not merely on the basis of an analogy with the productive worker, but through a direct assumption of the role of 'craftsman'. There is here a return to the pre-bourgeois, pre-capitalist meaning of art (Taylor, pp. 32–3) but with a specifically proletarian orientation. Dmitriev declared, 'The artist is now simply a constructor and technician, a leader and foreman' (Sherwood, 1971/2, p. 27) who masters the materials at his disposal in order to transform them into man-made objects.

The constructivists pushed this line of thought to its limit. Stepanova, Popova and Tatlin actually worked in textile factories in order to put the theories of 'production art' into practice (ibid., p. 30). Later the Futurists reached the logical limit of production art in their application of the artisanal conception to the forms of art themselves. The utilitarian impetus expressed itself in a formal commitment to the 'fact', the only kind of content worthy of the new age. The only artistic forms worthy of the factographic role were the newspaper report, the diary, the documentary film, and so on. By this stage the Futurists had negated their earlier negation of 'content'. It is clear that a transition had been effected from one notion of 'production' to another. But the new notion of 'production' did not mark the site of a genuine engagement with Marxism. 'Factography' was part of a reaction against the traditional mystified concept of 'art', and of an attempt to identify 'life' with 'art' in the new world in which industrial production had moved into the centre of life. But for Futurists and for Shklovsky, the *content* of the new art was indifferent. The ideology in which the factographer worked was simply a contingent fact.

The two notions of artistic production (one adopting form as its 'dominant', the other content) received their most extreme formulations in the Serapion Brothers' Credo of 1922 and in the purely instrumental aesthetics of Arvatov. In the former (Lev Lunc, Gruzdev, Kaverin), a total rejection of utility and uniformity is asserted very much in the spirit of the 1890s. Arvatov on the other hand reduced the notion of the artist's technical skill to a purely instrumental function (in response to the 'social command'). In reducing art to a branch of industry Arvatov was in effect denying art any autonomous status. Thus the rhetoric of material production could be made to jump either way.

At first (until about 1925) the Formalists' view of the ontological status of literature resembled the early Futurists' conception. Shklovsky's famous definition of a work of literature as 'the sum total of all stylistic devices employed in it' (Erlich, p. 90) displays the same mechanistic conception of art's materiality as one finds in Mayakovsky. The same anti-mimetic refusal of content is also present in Shklovsky's work. Form (the operation of the device) is the only content of art. Shklovsky's study of Sterne's *Tristram Shandy* brilliantly elaborated this argument. The novel is distinguished by the fact that 'The artistic form is presented simply as such, without any kind of motivation.' Sterne's refusal of 'content' justifies Shklovsky's claim that '*Tristram Shandy* is the most typical novel in world literature' (Lemon and Reis, pp. 27, 57). Shklovsky's inability to make a theoretical break with the Futurist hypostatisation of form is interestingly disclosed at a point where a break through looks possible in his discussion of the compositional status of 'sentimentality' in Sterne's novel:

> Art, then, is unsympathetic – or beyond sympathy – except where the feeling of compassion is evoked as material for the artistic structure. In discussing such emotion we have to examine it from the point of view of the composition itself, in exactly the same way that a mechanic must examine a driving [*sic*] belt to understand the details of a machine. (ibid., p. 44)

The resemblance to T. S. Eliot's theory of artistic impersonality is as striking as is the difference in the two critics' forms of expression. The comparison with the machine tends to negate the proto-structuralist suggestiveness of Shklovsky's discussion of the 'artistic structure'. The composition is rendered a static system. Nevertheless, the idea that extra-literary 'content' (compassion) is transformed into material for the artistic structure represents a very real advance on the cruder formalism of the Futurists. Shklovsky's retention of the artisanal model of artistic production has the advantage that it ensures demystification and specificity, but it limits literature's *mode* of materiality to that of the mechanical mode. The abandonment of the artisanal model by Tynyanov and later by the Prague School changed this.

Shklovsky's failure to transform a materialist rhetoric into a theoretical instrument is finally related to his conception of form. His separation of form and content was expressed as a distinction between the 'device' (*priem*) and 'motivation' (*motivirovka*). *Tristram Shandy* was remarkable for the fact that the literary devices were unmotivated and were simply 'bared'. It is more usual for the artistic devices to be justified in terms of 'life', for example by character, ideology, the destiny of the hero, the setting of the action. Thus the roles of form and content are reversed. Content exists in the work of art merely to sustain form. The ground is prepared here for a tactical volte-face: Shklovsky's response to Marxist criticisms of the Formalists' neglect of social content was to admit that the ideological motivations did indeed require investigation. In 1928 he produced a pragmatic synthesis of the sociological and the Formalist approaches in his *Materials and Style in Leo Tolstoy's War and Peace*, in which the novel is analysed in terms of a tension between 'class' and 'genre' (Erlich, pp. 122–5). Similarly Eichenbaum attempted a methodological compromise in his article 'Literature and Literary Mores' (1927). The abandonment of a commitment to the theoretical autonomy of the literary world marked a transition from a materialism which resided in the specific production of literary structures to a materialism which resided in the subordination of the superstructure to the base. The new sociological Formalism gave rise to studies of literary economics and the history of publishing, for example in *Literature and Commerce* (1927) by Gric, Trenin and Nikitin, a study of the Smirdin publishing house in the nineteenth century. On the other hand, in the same period, Voloshinov, Bakhtin and Medvedev were accommodating Marxism in a totally different way.

Formalism and Representation

The early Formalists were vehemently opposed to the representational basis of their predecessors' literary theory and practice. They followed the Futurists in asserting a revolutionary break with this tradition. In the new era art would create its own objects, not merely imitations of natural objects.

However, after the revolution a new interest in the semantic aspects of the verbal sign significantly altered the orientation of Formalist poetics. Shklovsky's use of the concept of 'defamiliarisation' (*ostranenie*) had important cognitive possibilities which should have attracted the attention of the Marxist critics. The poet's or novelist's deployment of literary devices does not simply give us back the familiar image of the world, but renews our perception of the world and of language. The obtrusiveness of the device in the literary structure forces the reader to abandon his 'automatised' perceptions and to perceive freshly the universe in all its 'density'. There is a remarkable similarity between Shklovsky's arguments and the Bergsonian theories of T. E. Hulme, the precursor of the Anglo-American New Criticism (cf. E. W. Thompson, pp. 66–7). He too argued that the poet renews our conventionalised perceptions. He too insisted on the rejection of the metaphysics of Romanticism and symbolism in favour of a new classical specificity and precision, which focused attention on language.

However it should be emphasised that for Shklovsky the renewal of perception served no cognitive function, but only a purely artistic function (see Della Volpe, p. 139). The device of defamiliarisation, argued Shklovsky, 'augments the difficulty and the duration of perception, since the process of perception in art is an end in itself and is supposed to be prolonged'. (Matejka and Pomorska, p. 13) Thus the devices of retardation in *Tristram Shandy*, of abbreviated or enlarged scale in *Gulliver's Travels* or of unexpected point of view in Tolstoy's *Kholstomer* (narrated by a horse) are not studied for their cognitive possibilities but simply as devices. The defamiliarisation effect was, so to speak, a by-product. In this respect Shklovsky's concept differs fundamentally from Brecht's alienation effect (see Jameson, p. 58; Mitchell) which not only gave rise to a de-automatisation of perception but also produced a cognitive effect. Shklovsky was uninterested in the ideological significance of defamiliarisation. In rigorously empirical fashion Shklovsky regards the objective universe as fixed and given. 'Reality' is static; only perception changes. Boris Tomashevsky exemplifies the ideological conservatism of early Formalism when he writes of the deeper levels of 'reality' as those 'general human interests (problems of love and death) which are the fixed bases of the entire course of human history'. (Lemon and Reis, p. 64) In Brecht the 'new reality' which presents itself to the artist requires the invention of new forms to comprehend it. Shklovsky is not interested in the nature of those conventional perceptions which the devices deform, nor in the cognitive significance of that deformation. The defamiliarisation device in *Gulliver's Travels* is not seen as being integrated into the ideological project; Swift's criticisms of English society are merely the motivation of the device. Shklovsky's discussion of Tolstoy's *Kholstomer* is particularly interesting in this respect. Noting that the narration from the horse's point of view 'makes the content of the story seem unfamiliar', he quotes a passage which shows how the horse regards the institution of private property (including 'There are people who call a tract of land their own but they never set eyes on it and never take a stroll on it'). However, Shklovsky draws attention not to the *perception* but to 'the manner of the narrative, its technique' (Lemon and Reis, pp. 14–15).

Trotsky had little patience with the anti-mimetic stance of the Futurists and Formalists; he was quick to point out that Formalism was not incompatible with representation:

> No one even thinks of asking the new literature to have a mirror-like impassivity. The deeper literature is, and the more it is imbued with the desire to shape life, the more significantly and dynamically it will be able to 'picture' life. (Trotsky, p. 137)

The concept of defamiliarisation proved more effective as a purely literary concept. In fact its immediate provenance was the Futurists' notion of the permanent revolution in the sphere of art. The renewal and redeployment of devices continually challenge the old literary order. Eichenbaum and Tynyanov began to apply the notion of defamiliarisation specifically to the history of the devices themselves. Thus old devices which have become familiar and automatised are made 'perceptible' again by being placed in a new context. Tynyanov's studies of parody (for example, *Dostoevsky and Gogol*, 1921) showed how the rather chaotic ideas of the Futurists and Shklovsky about the process of change in literary history could be reformulated in a way which opened the door to a genuinely materialist literary history, in the Formalist sense. We will take this up again later.

Formalism and the Notion of System

It has often seemed paradoxical that the historic hour of the revolution should also have been the timeless moment of the synchronic. The linguistics of Saussure is, of course, the best-known index of that moment. Saussure's distinction between the synchronic and the diachronic seems to have been the crucial factor influencing the Formalists' attribution of autonomy to the literary system.

In Saussure the *evolution* of a language is distinguished from the *system* which prevails at a particular (random) moment. The study of the former is diachronic, the latter synchronic linguistics. We can arrive at an understanding of the grammar of a language by taking an arbitrary segment, that is, by examining a particular *language-state*. Only by doing this can we study the relations between the elements in a language which compose its structure. Once we begin to consider historical changes which may have occurred in one or other element (changes in inflexions, or phonology) we lose sight of the static (synchronic) order which governs the language at any given moment. For a native speaker the language is a perfectly stable system at any given moment in time; the continual flux which language is undergoing is quite invisible to the speaker. Saussure summarised the point as follows:

> Language is a system whose parts can and must all be considered in their synchronic solidarity. Since changes never affect the system as a whole but rather one or another of its elements, they can be studied only outside the system. (Saussure, p. 87)

In so far as it supported the notion of the autonomy of literature the linguistics of Saussure were an influence on Shklovsky. But far from regarding literature as system(s) he conceived autonomy in terms of a poetry–prose distinction (compare Wordsworth, and I. A. Richards): poetry (literature) is distinguished by its deployment of devices in order to create a 'special perception' of the world. Jakobson's emphasis on autonomy was directly linguistic in conception: 'The real field of literary science is not literature but *literariness*.' While Shklovsky and Jakobson differed over the question of the relationship between a literary science and linguistics, they agreed in practice on the essentially synchronic nature of their enquiries. Richard Sherwood rightly argues that Shklovsky was interested in linguistics only in so far as it supported an intrinsic theory of art, and that this 'was a decisive factor in the a-historical attitude of early Russian Formalism' (Sherwood, 1973, p. 28).

From the point of view of Marxism, Shklovsky's conception of an autonomous literary science was questionable on several counts. First, the conception of the artistic work as the sum of the literary devices employed excluded the consideration of non-literary materials except in their role as 'motivation'. Secondly, Shklovsky's use of the concept of 'defamiliarisation' did nothing to readmit the historical series into the literary structure. Thirdly, any talk of 'autonomy' smacked of Kantian idealism and decadent bourgeois escapism. Many of these criticisms have real substance. The best known and probably the most theoretically sophisticated official criticism of the Formalists came from Trotsky in his *Literature and Revolution*. As has been often noticed, it was by no means totally negative.

Trotsky criticises the Formalist tendency to insist on the autonomy of the word, and points out the ahistorical nature of Shklovsky's notion of form. Trotsky produces a number of theses of his own which are of considerable interest: 'A new artistic form, taken in a large historic way, is born in reply to new needs. . . . Language, changed and complicated by urban conditions, gives the poet a new verbal material' (Trotsky, p. 167). Several criticisms made of Shklovsky are impressive, even if one is unsympathetic with Trotsky's insistence on the historic demand placed on art to express 'a new spiritual point of view'. In so far as Shklovsky's poetics resemble art for art's sake, Trotsky is on safe ground. While sustaining the essential Marxist doctrine of the ultimate social determination of all art (whether tendentious or 'pure'), Trotsky, in a celebrated passage, goes a long way to allowing the Formalists a role in the theory of art, when he declares that 'Artistic creation . . . is . . . a deflection, a changing and a transformation of reality, *in accordance*

with the peculiar laws of art.' This appears to contradict his earlier
argument that the Formalists should be content to acknowledge that
their methods had 'a merely subsidiary, serviceable and technical
significance' (pp. 175, 164). One must admit that, if by 'transformation of reality' Trotsky has in mind Shklovsky's theory of defamiliarisation, he would not be making a major concession to the
Formalists, but merely acknowledging the distorting effect of art and
not the cognitive power of that effect.

Whatever the real nature of Trotsky's remarks, they were con-
strued as a positive encouragement to those who sought a solution in
terms of a division of labour between the Formalists and the
Marxists. The former would elaborate those 'laws of art' which were
not the domain of Marxist theory, while the Marxists would theorise
the social structure. Eichenbaum's reply to the attacks of Kogan and
Lunacharsky in a symposium in *Press and Revolution* amounted to an
elaboration of Trotsky's conceded theory of separate spheres. He
insisted that no cultural phenomenon could be reduced to, or
derived from, social facts of a different order (*rjad*) (Erlich, p. 109).
Trotsky's most striking admission is directly concerned with
autonomy:

> It is very true that one cannot always go by the principles of
> Marxism in deciding whether to reject or to accept a work of
> art. A work of art should, in the first place, be judged by its
> own law, that is, by the law of art. But Marxism alone can
> explain why and how a given tendency in art has originated in
> a given period of history; in other words, who it was who made
> a demand for such an artistic form and not for another, and
> why. (Trotsky, p. 178)

Thus, if we leave aside the question of the cognitive power of art,
Trotsky is unequivocal in his admission that there is no Marxist
theory of art as such, but only a Marxist sociology of art. It is not
clear what Trotsky meant by 'the law of art', or whether he believed
that the elaboration of the science of literature would provide more
than a merely technical and therefore auxiliary function (as his
earlier remarks suggest). The call for a theory of art takes on a
different meaning if, like Louis Althusser, you do not regard art as
merely 'ideology' or expression of ideology. If Althusser is right in

believing that art (in its major achievements) offers us a realisation of ideology by achieving a 'retreat, an internal distantation' from the ideology out of which it emerged, then it becomes necessary to pursue a 'knowledge of art', even while admitting that Marxism itself will not afford such a knowledge. It seems to me that this position on the relation between Marxism and Formalism was implicit in some of the debates of the mid- and late 1920s. I would suggest that the failure to solve the problem was not entirely due to the hostility of the Russian Association of Proletarian Writers (RAPP) and the Proletkult group, but was at least partially the result of the theoretical limitation inherent in early Formalism. It is easy to be fatalistic about history and to say that once RAPP had been given its head and had been licensed to purge Soviet criticism, the work of the Formalists was doomed. It is true that the great theoretical advances achieved by Jakobson, Tynyanov, Bakhtin and Voloshinov at the end of the 1920s did not prevent the suppression of the Formalist project. But there is little doubt that the notion of Formalism which had crystallised in the minds of the official spokesmen was the Formalism of Shklovsky, which could be so easily regarded as the last vestige of a decadent aestheticism.

Formalism and the Problem of Synchrony and Diachrony

As we have seen, early antagonisms between Marxists and Formalists partly stemmed from Shklovsky's naïve empiricism and from his mechanical notion of artistic structure. While the concept of 'defamiliarisation' opens the possibility of a history of literature in terms of the successive replacements of artistic devices and the resulting renewal of 'perception', in Shklovsky's hands history dissolves into mere contingency and becomes re-internalised in the synchrony of the system. The solution of the problem required a theoretical perspective which would permit both the articulation of the literary and the extra-literary systems, and the overcoming of the contradiction between the synchronic and the diachronic.

The problem of the relation between the synchronic and the diachronic dimensions of a system has haunted the history of both Marxist and structuralist theory since the time of Saussure. Saussure himself appears to have recognised that there were at least two quite different ways of ordering the concepts. Synchrony may be conceived as either the universal system of rules which governs language(s), or the particular structuring of the elements at a given random moment. Even more significantly, diachrony may be either the history of the elements (their provenance or genesis), or the succession of synchronic moments which the structuralist reveals. The first view, which seeks a universal system and relegates diachrony to the status of an external precondition, is characteristic of the structuralism of Lévi-Strauss. The second view, which sees a structure not only in the static (synchronic) segment but also in the succession (diachrony) of such segments, was adopted by the later Formalists, notably Jakobson and Tynyanov.

These opposed views of system, which have very different implications for literary study, are illustrated in Saussure's two conflicting versions of the analogy between language and chess. In the first, the various stages of the game are regarded as synchronic moments, when the pieces are related in particular structural patterns. Each move leads to a new order. Diachrony is the *changed* condition of the elements, and is *given* at each stage. However, the 'rules' of the game ('the constant principles of semiology') exist before a game begins, and persist after each move. In the second version of the analogy, the rules of the game, which operate throughout the play, constitute the synchronic system; diachrony is reduced to the external provenance of the game (its history and origin). In this case, diachrony is simply the historical precondition of synchrony; Saussure says of language: 'The diachronic perspective deals with phenomena that are unrelated to systems although they do condition them.' The fact that the value of a particular piece may have changed during the history of the game does not directly affect the synchronic system but merely conditions it.

In the first version of the analogy, diachrony is the succession of synchronic moments – the dynamic, so to speak, of the game. The diachrony is subsumed (re-internalised) in the synchrony of the overall system. In the second version, diachrony is totally external to the dynamic of the system. Thus Saussure's ambivalence draws attention to two types of diachrony: the diachrony of accidental and external origins (the history of the game, the substance of the chess pieces, and so on), and the diachrony of the changes in the disposition of elements in a particular game's system. The first type has been essential to most structuralist theory, in which 'structure' is a timeless set of 'rules' whose transformations are conceived as being internally articulated within the realm of the synchronic. Such a structuralism asks no questions about the *genesis* of the elements in the system nor seeks to establish the *evolution* of the system which results from the modification and redeployment of elements.

In literary studies the inadequacies of an ahistorical, synchronic conception of the literary system have become apparent. The literary system is evidently one which has undergone continual structural modification and even revolution. Only the most socially mediated literary genres have been susceptible to strictly synchronic analysis. The less conventionalised (and 'open') literary forms are evidently less 'rule-governed'. What may work for Russian folk-tales may not work for a Shakespeare play.

The later period of Russian Formalism differs from the 'structuralist' poetics of Propp, Todorov, Greimas and others in its conception of the relation of synchrony and diachrony. Greimas described the history of literature as a succession of static systems (see Culler, 1975, pp. 75–95). The dominance of a genre in a particular period is seen as a process of working through and exhausting the transformations of a particular model or basic plot paradigm, which is then replaced by a new model. History is bracketed out: both the process of transition from one model of plot to another, and the historical conditioning of the elements within a given system are reduced to the status of external and unstructured preconditions.

The limitations of Saussure's chess analogy may now be appreciated. If one regards an individual game of chess as equivalent to a 'performance' according to an unchanging set of 'rules', the analogy might fit the universalist type of poetics, which aims to provide a generative grammar of literary narrative. But the analogy which compares the moves within a game with the synchronic stages in a diachronic succession will not work, because the disposition of chess pieces on the board at a given stage does not correspond to a total system operating at a given moment (in language or literature). The loss of particular pieces from the board in no way corresponds to the alteration or mutation of elements in a total system. A more appropriate analogy would be the succession of historical periods during which particular systems of rules are in operation. Synchrony would then become the system of rules prevailing in one such period.

But even this analogy will not work for the literary system. In the linguistic system, the changes which condition the synchronic states may affect phonology, syntax or semantics. According to Saussure, the etymology of a word (its past history) will condition the word's function in the language system, but does not have *direct* bearing on the word's place and function in the system. The fact that the word 'presently' has changed its meaning since the Elizabethan period does not affect the word's functioning in modern English. But, in the literary system, the past history of a word as literary sign *does* affect its functioning in the system. While it is possible to consider the literary system synchronically as an 'ideal order' composed of all the literary materials available at a given historical moment, the 'history' of the materials cannot be relegated to the status of the system's preconditions.

These difficulties of a formalist or structural notion of a system were recognised and solved in two quite different ways by Jakobson and Tynyanov and by the Bakhtin school. The first solution was to break down the rigid antithesis between synchrony and diachrony and to place on the agenda a theory of the historical articulation of 'systems'. The second approach was to reject the whole Saussurean notion of a synchronic system and to replace it with a theory of a changeable and adaptable sign system whose focus becomes the social context of utterances. The first approach anticipates Althusser's complex ideas on structural causality; the second influenced post-structuralist theories of the 'speaking subject'.

In the brief 'Theses on Formalism' written by Jakobson and Tynyanov in 1928 for *Novyi Lef*, the dialogue between Marxism and Formalism, which was at an antagonistic stage in Shklovsky's work, was raised to a new level. While acknowledging the theoretical importance of the linguistic conception of synchrony, they insisted that 'the history of a system is in turn a system'. 'Pure synchronism now proves to be an illusion: every synchronic system has its past and its future as inseparable structural elements in the system.' (Matejka and Pomorska, p. 79) The prerequisite of this new conception of structure was the abandonment of Shklovsky's mechanistic model (the work as an aggregate of devices) in favour of a dynamic model. As early as 1924 Tynyanov wrote: 'The unity of a literary work is not that of a closed symmetrical whole, but . . . of a dynamic integration. . . . The form of the literary work must be described as dynamic' (Erlich, p. 90). The dynamism is admitted into the structure through the concept of the 'dominant', the focusing component of a work which governs and orders other components and guarantees the integrity of the entire structure. The importance of the dynamic model of structure is felt not only in the poetics of the individual work, but particularly in the diachronic dimension of the system. The evolution of the literary system is conceived now as the redeployment of elements (of form and content) which have previously been used for a different function. In one period a particular formal feature may be used 'seriously', but in another it is defamiliarised in the context of parody. Certain elements are promoted to the 'foreground' in a particular work, while others, which may have previously had a dominant function, are relegated to the background. Jakobson concluded:

> In the evolution of poetic form it is not so much a question of the disappearance of certain elements and the emergence of others, as it is the question of shifts in the mutual relationship among the diverse components of the system, in other words, a question of the shifting dominant. (Matejka and Pomorska, p. 85)

The notion of the 'dominant' (later called 'foregrounding' by the Prague School) enables the theorist to escape from a confining synchronic view of system. As in T. S. Eliot's theory of tradition, the concept of innovation is situated in a dynamic historical context:

> It is precisely against the background of [the traditional canon] that innovation is conceived. The formalist studies brought to light that this simultaneous preservation of tradition and breaking away from tradition form the essence of every new work of art. (p. 87)

The abandoning of a rather positivistic notion of literary science and of the work of art was encouraged by the German tradition of *Ganzheit* and *Gestalt*, wholeness and totality, and by Husserl's phenomenology. The problems about form and content which had preoccupied Shklovsky and others were resolved without requiring either the reduction of 'content' to non-intrinsic, non-aesthetic materials, or the total absorption of content to form.

The work of Jan Mukařovský marks a decisive shift towards a

sociological explanation of the literary system. He developed Jakobson's and Tynyanov's concept of the 'dominant' in such a way as to produce a much more social and relativistic view of the literary. He used the term 'aesthetic function' to describe a changing and adjustable domain within the larger social system. The aesthetic and the extra-aesthetic are spheres whose relationship is constantly being modified, enlarging and shrinking in response to larger social pressures and conditions. An aesthetic canon is always relative to the social organisation in which it arises. 'There are no objects or actions', he argues, 'which, by virtue of their essence or organization, would, regardless of time, place or the person evaluating them, possess an aesthetic function' (Mukařovský, p. 1). He made a decisive break with the Formalists' concept of system and with any hint of Kantianism. Indeed, Raymond Williams regards Mukařovský's writings as a major contribution to 'the critical dissolution of the specializing and controlling categories of bourgeois aesthetic theory' (Williams, 1977, p. 153). Tony Bennett and later Terry Eagleton have also adopted a historically relativised view of the literary which resembles Mukařovský's (see also Kavanagh). According to these writers, the field of literature is always contested; literary works are appropriated, reappropriated, dissolved and reconstructed, according to the cultural practices prevailing at the moment of reception. There is no literary system except in a purely transient and reified sense. From this point of view, the reception of texts is the determining instance in the chain of communication. The concept of innovation ceases to have any objective status: traditions and literary canons undergo perpetual challenge and reconstruction; and traditions are always selective, since changes in the social order both readjust the border between the 'literary' and the 'extra-literary', *and* redefine the ideological positioning of particular works.

The concept of selective tradition is a valuable one. Seen as an aspect of ideological struggle, any selective tradition invites a counter selection: one can trace fascinating sequences of traditions and counter-traditions (those, for example, constructed by Arnold, Leavis and Raymond Williams). However we also need an objective form of tradition, consisting of a *history of those innovating moments* which produced dislocations and readjustments in the literary field. Such a 'tradition' would have both a diachronic and a synchronic dimension: it is both an evolution and, at its latest moment, a summation of the relations between the innovative moments. To abandon the possibility of achieving a knowledge of tradition in this sense would be to abandon the project envisaged but interrupted at the end of the 1920s in Russia.

The most striking theoretical formulation made in the Jakobson–Tynyanov theses is contained in the final paragraph, where it is conceded that a knowledge of the 'immanent laws of the history of literature' does not explain the specific determination of literary evolution (that is, why one specific evolutionary path was followed and not another):

> The question of a specific choice of path, or at least of the dominant, can be solved only by means of an analysis of the correlation between the literary series and other historical series. This correlation (a system of systems) has its own structural laws, which must be submitted to investigation. (Matejka and Pomorska, pp. 80–1)

In order to prevent any misunderstandings, the paragraph concludes: 'It would be methodologically fatal to consider the correlation of systems without taking into account the immanent laws of each system.' It is left unspecified which body of theory would undertake the investigation of the system of systems. Althusser's reading of Marx suggests that the essential Marxist contribution to knowledge is the inauguration of the science of history conceived precisely in terms of a knowledge of a complex 'social whole' composed of 'levels' or 'instances' articulated by a structure of determination. On this reading, a Marxist history investigates the structural laws of the system of levels, while the structural laws of literature (art) require a separate theorising consistent with the relative autonomy of the literary system.

Before we proceed to discuss Marx's and Engels's views, it should be noted that the 'structuralist' conception of history developed by Althusser differs in an important way from that sketched in the Jakobson–Tynyanov theses, and affects the issue of diachrony–synchrony. In Althusser there is a Lévi-Straussian commitment to the synchronic: '*The synchronic is eternity in Spinoza's sense,* or the adequate knowledge of a complex object by the adequate knowledge of its complexity.' (Althusser, 1970, p. 107) He rejects the empiricist notion of 'diachrony' as the 'sequence of events' which, he argues, abandons history to the accidental and the contingent. In his view diachrony is a purely epistemological concept, alluding to the order in which the concepts succeed one another within historical knowledge itself. Thus diachrony is incorporated within the timeless domain of the synchronic. While Althusser's attack upon the empiricist notion of 'historical time' as 'homogeneous-continuous' and 'self-contemporaneous' is convincing, his admission of historicity into the particular 'levels' within the social whole does not go as far as permitting the idea of a diachronic evolution but only of relative degrees of development (retarded or advanced) of the levels in relation to one another.

Marx and Engels on 'Art'

In considering the Marx of Louis Althusser, the Marxist aesthetician or literary critic is confronted by a profound dilemma. It would seem that s/he must either consign the comments of Marx (and Engels) on art to the limbo of an ideological pre-history, or re-establish the image of an eclectic, non-scientific Marx who unites in his ample embrace the materialist, idealist and humanist streams of Western European thought. The problem is especially acute for the theorist of the arts, since Marx's own pronouncements are almost exclusively expressed in the concepts of his idealist and humanist phases. For Roger Garaudy (pp. 177 ff.) the Paris Manuscripts are the key to Marxist aesthetics. Mikhail Lifshitz draws particularly on the early Marx for central aesthetic concepts ('alienation', 'measure', the genesis of the aesthetic sense, 'realism'). Even the later notions of 'typicality' and 'tendentiousness' cannot easily be rescued from the clutches of an ideological 'problematic'.

The writings on art by Marx and Engels do not appear to encourage us to attempt a *rapprochement* between Formalism and Marxism. Like Plato, Marx did not set forth a systematic account of the nature of art and its relations with the social formation as a whole. The various casual remarks are often in the form of informal letters or polemical reviews. The 'aesthetics' which have been deduced from this material (by Lifshitz, Demetz, Morawski) have been constructed on the premise that art is an ideological product rather than a partially autonomous practice requiring its own theoretical practice (criticism). I would argue that a 'knowledge' of art is required by the Marxist problematic (historical materialism), but is not provided in the corpus of classic texts (except in one or two hints, discussed below).

It is true that Marx never effected a transition from pre-Marxist aesthetic concepts (Schiller, Hegel, Winckelmann) to a theoretical practice adequate to the new problematic (the science of history) which underlines his mature work. However, the 'specific effectivity' of ideological practices is implied in innumerable passages even where the dominance of the economic is heavily stressed. The following extract from *The German Ideology* is characteristic:

> [We have] to show it [civil society] in its action as State, to explain all the different theoretical products and forms of consciousness, religion, philosophy, ethics, etc. etc. and trace their origins and growth from that basis; by which means, of course, the whole thing can be depicted in its totality (and therefore, too, the reciprocal action of these various sides on one another). It has not, like the idealistic view of history, in every period to look for a category, but remains constantly on the real *ground* of history; it does not explain practice from the idea but explains the formation of ideas from material practice. (Marx, 1970, p. 58)

The formation of ideas is 'explained' by those material conditions (productive forces, and so on) which are handed on by the predecessors of each generation and which are modified by each generation. However, the 'whole thing' is conceived as a 'totality', not of the simple Hegelian kind ('a category in every historical period') but of a *complex* nature involving 'reciprocal action'. A sentence of Althusser's might well have been commenting on the passage: 'Marxism conceives the "conditions" as the (real, concrete, current) existence of the contradictions that constitute the whole of the historical process.' (Althusser, 1971, p. 209) The significance of this aspect of the Marxist totality was elucidated by Engels in the famous letters of the 1890s.

Most non-Marxist interpreters now recognise that Marx's socio-economic determinism is at the very least ambiguous. Most commentators like to contrast Marx's hard-line deterministic formulations of the 1840s and 1850s with the later alleged equivocations or dilutions of Engels. Peter Demetz, for example, argues that Engels's well-known discussion of the formula in the letters to Joseph Bloch and Conrad Schmidt contradicts the earlier versions of the theory of economic determinism:

> He thought he was talking about only a more sensitive application of the immutable principles of dialectical materialism, whereas the implications of his interpretations were clearly beginning to erode the absolute primacy of economics in human affairs. (Demetz, p. 142)

The crucial passage in Engels is as follows:

> Political, legal, philosophical, religious, literary and artistic development rest on the economic. But they also react on each other and on the economic base. It is not that the economic factor is the only active factor and everything else mere passive effect, but it is the interaction with the economic base which always proves decisive in the last analysis.

It might seem possible to take the view that Engels here sells the pass by compromising the main principle. Engels seems to admit this when he says 'Marx and I are ourselves partly to blame for the fact that the younger people sometimes lay more stress on the economic side than is due to it. We had to emphasise the main principle vis-à-vis our adversaries, who denied it.' Engels's rejection of a mechanical application of 'the main principle' is welcomed by Thomas Monro as 'a moderate statement' which

> if accepted by present communist theoreticians, would go far toward making the Marxist view of art history acceptable in Western eyes. It retains Marx's essential contribution, but moves substantially toward the pluralism of Taine. (Monro, p. 439)

Happy motivation! Even Demetz saw that there is no way of accommodating Taine with even the late Engels. As Demetz puts

it, 'Engels stubbornly continues to believe in the ultimate self-realisation of the economic impulses, whereas Taine considers the
economic element one of many elements in the "aggregate" that
determines the development of the arts' (p. 150). Far from being
either a 'moderate statement' or an erosion of the primacy of the
economic, Engels's formulation of the base-superstructure theory is
an important clarification of the Marxist theory of the social formation as a whole.

The argument for economic determinism as set forth in Marx's
and Engels's *The German Ideology* is the natural starting-point for an
investigation since this work marks the first complete break with
their Hegelian philosophical past and presents the kind of vigorous
polemic against the Hegelians which Engels evidently had in mind
when he referred to their having had to emphasise the 'main point'
with their adversaries.

Indeed there are clear signs that the determinism of the famous
passages on ideology are positivistic in tendency rather than Marxist.
The exuberant metaphoric display ('ideological reflexes and echoes',
'phantoms formed in the human brain', 'sublimations', 'circumstances appear upside down in all ideology as in a camera obscura')
suggest that Marx was at the stage of theoretical antithesis and was
without an adequate model (metaphor) for his new formulation of
totality. Nevertheless his rather polemical statement that ideology
has no 'history', and no 'development' has been too flippantly mis-
interpreted. For example, Demetz argues that the (humanistic) hopes
raised by an 'unexpected stress upon the "real life-process" . . . are
brutally disappointed by their effort to rob the human spirit – and
with it the poetic imagination – of any autonomous energy'. It must
be stressed that no understanding of the apparently reductive
formula 'Consciousness does not determine life; life determines
consciousness' is possible without reference to the polemical context
of the remark in the debate with Feuerbach and the Young Hegelians.
The philosophical and the political issues are inseparable: Marx and
Engels argue that the Young Hegelians do not go beyond Hegel in so
far as they fail to recognise the priority of the 'real life-processes' of
human beings. The Young Hegelians believe that human consciousness and all its products (thoughts, ideas) have an independent
existence and constitute the real chains which limit human development:

Since, according to their fantasy, the relationships of men, all
their doings, their chains and their limitations are products of
their consciousness, the Young Hegelians logically put to men
the moral postulate of exchanging their present consciousness
for human, critical or egoistic consciousness, and thus of removing their limitations. (Marx, 1970, p. 41)

The implication is clear: we cannot change human consciousness at
will, because consciousness is not an independent and autonomous
reality. We can understand human beings' consciousness (the
development of their ideas) only 'on the basis of their real life processes', and, by implication, no *revolution* in human consciousness
can occur except on the same basis.

C. J. Arthur's introduction to *The German Ideology* offers a further
valuable corrective to reductive views of the text:

It is possible to select certain one-sided formulations, which
the authors no doubt resorted to for the purpose of contrasting
forcibly their positions from those of the dominant idealist
trends, and make these the basis of a fatalistic view which
negates human purposefulness and activity. This kind of view
is sometimes referred to as 'mechanistic materialism', since its
categories are homologous with those with which natural
science treats its objects.

A careful reading of Marx's work soon shows that this interpretation is not adequate; because the circumstances which are
held to shape and form consciousness are not independent of
human activity. They are precisely the *social* relations which
have been *historically* created by human action. (Marx, 1970,
pp. 21–2)

In the light of this, it makes more sense to regard Engels's comments
of 1890 not as erosion of the main principle but as an important
clarification of the implications of historical materialism for the
superstructural elements. Both the early and late writings are a
repudiation of 'mechanical materialism'. The most that might be
conceded to the critic is that by boldly inverting the formula
'consciousness determines life' Marx and Engels were oversimplify-
ing or obscuring the theoretical assumptions underlying their

materialism for the sake of polemical effectiveness. A similar polemical overemphasis in William Blake's opposition between Imagination and Reason has led to a neglect of the dialectical subtlety of Blake's argument. The polemic against 'reason' was part of a dialectical dynamic which cannot be understood outside Blake's critique of the dominant neo-classical rationalism of the third quarter of the eighteenth century.

Marx recognised intellectual work as a distinct kind of labour, and criticised others for not doing so or for neglecting the historical forms of such work. In a passage in the *Theory of Surplus Value* Marx criticises Storch's and Adam Smith's theories of the relations between material and intellectual labour. For Smith intellectual labour is unproductive if it is does not contribute directly to production: 'In intellectual production another kind of labour appears productive. But Smith does not consider it.' Storch, on the other hand, is unable to locate his argument in the context of a definite historical form of production:

> the kind of intellectual production corresponding to capitalist methods of production is different from that corresponding to medieval methods of production. If material production itself is not grasped in its specific historical form, it is impossible to understand the concrete nature of the intellectual production corresponding to it and the interplay of both factors. (Marx and Engels, 1947, p. 24)

While recognising that intellectual production is a distinct kind of productive labour, Marx does not have at his disposal the necessary theoretical concepts with which to produce a knowledge of art, and falls back upon the Hegelian inheritance in seeing a contradiction between capitalism and 'certain aspects of intellectual production, such as art and poetry' (for example, bourgeois society cannot produce epics). His remarks have some relevance to a 'sociology of art' but do not point towards a knowledge of artistic labour.

Engels, in his letter to Conrad Schmidt (27 October 1890), discusses intellectual production (specifically philosophy) in similarly suggestive terms:

> the philosophy of every epoch, since it is a definite sphere in the division of labour, has as its presupposition certain definite

intellectual material handed down to it by its predecessors, from which it takes its start . . . economy creates nothing absolutely new (*a novo*), but determines the way in which the existing material of thought is altered and further developed, and that, too, for the most part indirectly, for it is the political, legal and moral reflexes which exercise the greatest direct influence upon philosophy. (Marx and Engels, 1947, p. 6)

This passage qualifies and interprets for us a crux in *The German Ideology* ('no history, no development'). The transformation of certain definite intellectual material is conditioned by the specific historical form of material production.

In the early Hegelian 'Comments on the Latest Prussian Censorship Instruction' (1842), Marx mocks the censor's insistence on the 'restrained pursuit of truth':

truth is universal. It does not belong to me, it belongs to all; it possesses me, I do not possess it. A *style* is my property, my spiritual individuality. *Le style, c'est l'homme.* Indeed! The law permits me to write, only I am supposed to write in a style different from *my own*. (Marx, 1967, p. 71)

The concept of style here remains within the realm of romantic idealism: style is an expression of spirit (albeit individual spirit). A quite different concept of style appears in Marx's and Engels's long book-review of Carlyle's *Latter Day Pamphlets* (1850). Before launching an attack on Carlyle's anti-proletarian views, the reviewers pay tribute to his earlier style:

As with Carlyle's ideas, so with his style. It is a direct and violent reaction against the modern bourgeois English Pecksniff style, whose stilted superficiality, circumspect verbosity and confused moral-sentimental tediousness has spread from its original inventors, the educated Cockneys, over all English literature. By contrast, Carlyle handles the English language as if it were completely *raw material which he has to recast from the ground up*. Archaic words and expressions are revived and new ones invented in the German manner. . . . This new style was often over-inflated and tasteless, but at times brilliant and always original. (Marx and Engels, 1947, p. 104, my emphasis)

The literary world is here conceived of as a *practice* involving the transformation of a material into a product (a 'new style'). Carlyle's early work is an intervention in what Engels called 'the struggle of ideas', but at the same time it is a *stylistic* struggle. The revolution in consciousness is also a revolution in style. Carlyle's creation of a 'new style' from the materials of tradition is described in a totally demystified idiom, quite remote from Buffon's famous reification ('le style c'est l'homme même') which Marx had echoed in idealistic fashion in the earlier text. Carlyle's style is original in its transformation of the language on the basis of specific materials (archaic expressions and neologisms in the manner of Jean-Paul Richter).

Surveying the texts of Marx one can distinguish the presence of at least three conceptions of art. The first, which predominates in the early Marx, has two forms: idealistic-Utopian and humanistic-sensuous. The former is dependent on the romantic view of art as a perfection transcending the 'realm of necessity' (Schiller). The latter form is dependent on a Feuerbachian view of man as 'species-being', an abstract type of humanism which Marx criticised in *The German Ideology*.

The idealist-Utopian conception of art appears in the *Grundrisse* in the famous discussion of 'uneven development':

> In the case of the arts, it is well known that certain periods of their flowering are out of all proportion to the general development of society, hence also to the material foundation, the skeletal structure as it were, of its organisation. (Marx, 1973, p. 110)

Marx is drawing on the tradition of German idealism ('it is well known') in recognising an autonomous realm of art. The 'perfection' of Greek art called for an explanation even within an Hegelian developmental model, but within a Marxian model of social dialectic a more difficult problem was raised:

> Certain significant forms within the realm of the arts are possible at an underdeveloped stage of artistic development. If this is the case with the relation between different kinds of art within the realm of the arts, it is already less puzzling that it is the case in the relation of the entire realm to the general development of society. (p. 110)

The autonomy of art envisaged here is the autonomy of a perfect realm. However, Marx goes on to introduce an important qualification to this autonomy. Greek art is historically conditioned in so far as its existence is inconceivable in a social order 'which excludes all mythological, all mythologizing relations to nature; which therefore demands of the artist an imagination not dependent on mythology' (p. 110). However, Marx goes on to raise what for him represented a greater difficulty, namely, how it is that Greek arts and epic 'still afford us artistic pleasure and that in a certain respect they count as a norm and as an unattainable model' (p. 111). Behind this question lie Hegelian aesthetic assumptions about art as an expression of freedom and as a spiritual essence to be found in an unalienated state in Greek culture (Prawer, pp. 280–9). Marx's answer to the question is pure Hegel: 'Why should not the historical childhood [in Hegel, adolescence] of humanity, its most beautiful unfolding, as a stage never to return, exercise an eternal charm?'

There have been several interpretations of the abrupt breaking off of the manuscript at this point. According to Demetz Marx realised that his economic determinism was in conflict with his good taste. In my view, the theory of 'uneven development' hides an unresolved problem: the autonomy accorded to the realm of art is characterised here by a Kantian disinterestedness and a *freies Spiel der Seelenkrafte*, a conception which seals 'art' from the social formation in a thoroughly unMarxian fashion. Despite the promise of historical specificity in Marx's references to the development of 'certain significant forms within the realm of the arts', the conception remains idealist: particular modes of art are reduced to a reified 'art'. In the same passage in the *Grundrisse* Marx lays the foundations of modern sociology of art production (Berger, Benjamin, Williams) when he argues that 'art production' (that is, the professionalisation of art as a result of the division of labour) is incompatible with the development of certain art forms such as epic. However, this discussion also remains firmly within an idealist (Hegelian) problematic: an aesthetic perfection is no longer attainable under the alienated conditions of feudal or bourgeois society.

Deriving ultimately from the same idealist roots (Schiller, Kant), Marx's reflections on the genesis of art in the *1844 Manuscripts* are in the form of an aesthetic anthropology. The aesthetic sense is seen as having evolved during the historical evolution of labour. Primitive people develop and refine their aesthetic sense while shaping their work skills, all the while affirming their 'human essence' in the process: 'Hence the objectivisation of human existence, both in a theoretical and practical way, means making man's *senses human* as well as creating human *senses* corresponding to the vast richness of human and natural life.' Unlike animals, human beings produce universally, 'according to the measure of every species' and 'according to the laws of beauty'. Human beings produce 'independently of physical needs and really [produce] only when free of these needs'. (Marx and Engels, 1947, p. 13) This aesthetic view of human productive powers reappears in *Das Kapital* where Marx describes the effects of capitalistic manufacture: 'It converts the labourer into a crippled monstrosity, by forcing his detailed dexterity at the expense of a world of productive capabilities and instincts.' (Marx and Engels, 1947, p. 20) The Feuerbachian materialism of the *1844 Manuscripts* is rejected in *The German Ideology* together with Feuerbach's conception of human nature:

> He [Feuerbach] never arrives at the really existing active men, but stops at the abstraction 'man', and gets no further than recognising the 'true, individual, corporeal man' emotionally, i.e. he knows no other 'human relationships' 'of man to man' than love and friendship, and even then idealised. (Marx, 1970, p. 64)

The sixth thesis on Feuerbach, especially the rejection of Feuerbach's view of 'the essence of man merely as "species", as the inner dumb generality which unites the many individuals naturally', marks the close of Marx's preoccupation with an aesthetic anthropology.

The concept of 'sensuousness' (grasped only in abstract form by Feuerbach) remained an important aesthetic criterion throughout Marx's work. Greek art's perfection was bound up with its individuality and sensuousness. In contrast, bourgeois society produces the 'super-sensuous' realm of the commodity market: fetishism is associated with brutal formlessness. Classical 'measure' (*Mass*) is in contrast with the 'measurelessness' of capitalism.

'Sensuousness' becomes a prominent criterion of realism. In the review of Chenu's *Les Conspirateurs* (1850) it is argued that revolutionary leaders have never been depicted 'in their real form', 'in strong Rembrandtian colours, in all their living qualities' (Marx and Engels, 1947, p. 35). Both Marx and Engels, in their respective letters to Lasalle on his play *Franz von Sickingen*, advocate the realism of Shakespeare against the idealism of Schiller. Engels considers that the German theatre lacks 'Shakespearian vivacity'; the actions of Lasalle's main characters are given a sound historical motivation but 'these motives' should have been 'more lively, active'. The play's neglect of 'the unofficial plebian and peasants elements' is also associated with a general abstraction and lack of realism (ibid., pp. 40–9). The connection between a sensuous realism and a proletarian perspective is implied in Engels's later remarks on the poet George Weerth ('the first and *most important* poet of the German proletariat'), who was the master 'in expressing natural robust sensuousness and the joys of the flesh' (ibid., pp. 98–9).

The advocacy of sensuous realism and of the liberation of the human senses from the crippling effect of a world of commodity production had an immense ideological value in redefining the social orientation of humanism. But the genesis of a Marxist humanism and the supervening of a bourgeois humanism is not the basis of a theoretical practice. The classical Marxist concepts of 'mode of production' and social 'totality' do not, I believe, discourage the development of a 'materialist' literary criticism, even though the intellectual conditions for such a development were not present in the nineteenth century.

'Relative Autonomy'

Althusser's attempt to rethink the base and superstructure problem was partly anticipated in the semiotic Marxism of Bakhtin, Voloshinov and Medvedev, who attempted to assimilate the Formalists' practices to a larger enterprise (Medvedev calls it a 'sociological poetics'), which recognises that literature is an autonomous 'branch' of ideology possessing its own distinctively structured system. Works of literature do not simply reflect other branches of ideology (ethical, cognitive, and so on), but 'have an autonomous ideological role and a type of refraction of socio-economic existence entirely of their own.' (Titunik, p. 180) Althusser goes beyond the position of Voloshinov and Bakhtin in relation to ideology. Art (in its major instances) gives us a fully realised 'perception' of ideology (not actually a 'knowledge' of ideology). The notion of relative autonomy here takes on a new significance and makes the brief *rapprochement* between Marxism and Formalism between 1928 and 1930 all the more pertinent to current problems in cultural studies.

It should be acknowledged that the notions of the 'system of systems' and of the dialectic of intrinsic and extrinsic materials, which offered a solution to the conflict between synchronic and diachronic dimensions and between structural and genetic explanations of art, have never been fully worked out in practice. It is all too easy, for example, to slip from a monistic conception into a pluralistic one. Althusser's reading of Marx has often been accused of this slippage. The problem is posed vividly in the work of Claudio Guillén, who accepted fully the doctrine of levels (structure, specificity, integration), and declared that 'Our real literary historian, like the student of cultures, is a "structural diachronicist"' (p. 507). But he proceeds to ask whether the historian should adopt a 'domination model' or an 'interaction model' of the relations between levels. Being a good liberal he is naturally inclined to the latter!

The phrase 'a system of systems' has a dauntingly mechanistic ring to it. However, in the form given to us by Althusser, it constitutes a very important model of historical theory. All totalising theories run the risk of a whole gamut of -isms, including essentialism, reductionism and idealism. In Anglo-American literary criticism the only type of totalising theory which has been found acceptable is the historicist variety. The literary productions of a period are assumed to be either part of the 'spirit of the age' or, more specifically, expressions of 'unit ideas' or the dominant intellectual tendencies of an age. Totality is only thinkable in terms of the centrality of the human 'mind' which radiates and expresses itself in all aspects of human life and culture. The inverse form of such totalising theory is a mechanical materialism which reduces human life in all its forms to a reflex of certain material agents, biological, geographical or socioeconomic. Faced with the options provided by Hegelian idealism or mechanical materialism it is tempting to abandon all totalising historical theories. However, Althusser's major contribution to the philosophy of history was his brilliant elaboration of a Marxist concept of totality which avoids the pitfalls of reductionism and essentialism, and at the same time preserves as its problematic a theory of the 'social formation as a whole'.

Althusser's concepts of 'structure in dominance', 'overdetermination' and 'relative autonomy' effect a displacement of the centre of history. Starting from the Marxist distinction between 'base' and 'superstructure', Althusser developed a subtle formulation of their relationship. Without abandoning the essential Marxist idea that life determines consciousness, he took up certain (now celebrated) late statements of clarification made by Engels, and produced a version of totality which preserved determinations but allowed their structure to be decentred. The economic level ceases to be the essential determinant, except in the 'last instance'; the ideological and political 'instances' are not simply reflections or reflexes of the economic instance but possess their own level of 'effectivity': 'on the one hand, determination in the last instance by the (economic) mode of production; on the other, the relative autonomy of the superstructures and their specific effectivity' (Althusser, 1969, p. 111). Althusser analysed the social formation as a whole in terms of three 'instances', the economic, the political and the ideological. Each has its own specific development and internal dialectics of conflict and contradiction, and yet each is acted upon by the developments taking place on the other levels. Thus, the social formation is *overdetermined*, in the sense that it is produced by and produces a number of relatively autonomous practices. The economic level never dominates the structure as a centre or essence:

> the economic dialectic is never active *in the pure state*; in History, these instances, the superstructures, etc. – are never seen to step respectfully aside when their work is done or, when the Time comes, as his pure phenomena, to scatter before His Majesty the Economy as he strides along the royal road of the Dialectic. From the first moment to the last, the lonely hour of 'the last instance' never comes. (p. 113)

The whole is thus *decentred* and is conceived as a 'structure in dominance': in particular historical periods the contradictions within a specific ideological practice (say, religion in the medieval period) may be dominant within the total formation, and yet *its* dominance is *in the last instance* assigned by the economic level.

Paul Hirst, in an influential discussion of Althusser's essay on Ideological State Apparatuses (ISAs), rejects the concept of relative autonomy. In his view the functionalism of the essay creates difficulties for Althusser's earlier theory of structural determinations. Hirst argues that his account of the reproduction of the relations of production is finally economistic; the unity of the ISAs is determined by the ruling class politics and ideology, which are, in turn, determined by the ruling class, itself an auto-existing instance. Hirst believes that Althusser is unable to transcend a theory of 'representation' that requires an ultimate objectivity of economic relations. He also believes that the theses of the 'relative autonomy of the superstructures' and 'reciprocal action of the base' complicate but do not alter the economism (Hirst, p. 53). I would wish to defend Althusser's earlier formulations by relating them to ideology at a more specific and historical level than is attempted in the ISAs essay. Laclau's development of Althusser's account of 'interpellation' of subjects (to be discussed below) is not functionalist: it argues that class ideologies have no class-belonging, and that they are produced by the synthesising of ideological materials of diverse kinds. Viewed in this way, the process of 'condensation' has, I suggest, an autonomous level of action, but is *related to* and ultimately subordinate to a larger structure. This is *not* covert economism, but an essential theoretical distinction between specific modes and forms of a process (a discourse) and the ultimate economic 'ground' which determines (but never finally) the relations between a process and the social formation as a whole. The concept of 'relative autonomy' is admittedly extremely general, and its explanatory power can be established only in the course of the elaboration of specific historical conjunctures.

Numerous criticisms of Althusser's model have been made, arguing that overdetermination is simply a covert form of pluralism, or that the theory is vitiated by the unsatisfactoriness of the base–superstructure dichotomy itself. It is certainly true that Althusser failed to go beyond a purely philosophical intervention and attempt to develop new readings of history. However, he certainly placed on the agenda a new model for historical studies which would involve the articulation of distinct regions of knowledge. Such knowledges would attempt to trace the structure of determinations which produced and were produced by particular social formations. We have had some ambitious historical overviews (see Anderson, 1974a,

1974b) and an impressive attempt by Terry Eagleton to rewrite the Great Tradition in Althusserian terms (Eagleton, 1976). However, the full implications of 'relative autonomy' for the aesthetic region of ideology are still not apparent.

As we have seen, Althusser places art in an intermediate space between 'knowledge' and 'ideology'. While minor writers or artists produce works which merely reflect other dominant ideological practices, others of a greater power produce texts or artefacts which give us not a conceptual knowledge but a distantiated perception or 'view' of ideology.

Eagleton has insisted that a science of literature can be constituted only in terms of the articulation of authorial and aesthetic ideologies into the hegemonic ideology as a whole. His critique of Althusser (whose influence is felt throughout Eagleton's *Criticism and Ideology*) is crucial to his argument. In Eagleton's view, both Althusser and Macherey are guilty of wanting to redeem the 'text' from 'the shame of the sheerly ideological' (p. 84). Eagleton rightly asks 'If "real" art is not to be ranked among the ideologies, does it then form a distinct region within the social formation?' He goes on to criticise Althusser, who by talking of 'authentic' and 'real' art introduces an evaluative judgement elicitly into 'what purports to be a scientific account of the structures of art as such'. He criticises Macherey for suggesting that the 'internal distantiation' from ideology achieved in the text is 'the effect of the form which the text bestows on ideology'. In a characteristically refined piece of logical ordering, Eagleton defines the relations between 'form' and 'ideology':

> It is not, naturally, as though form vanquished the inchoate-
> ness of ideology – a proposition parallel to the bourgeois
> critical assumption that art orders the 'chaos' of experience.
> Ideology is a relatively coherent formation, which thus broadly
> determines those structural definitions and distributions of
> meaning we term literary form; but the forms of the text are
> not, on the other hand, mere epiphenomena of an ideological
> 'content'. The form of the ideological content – the categorial
> structure of the ideological problematic – has a *generally*
> determining effect on the form of the text, not least in the
> determination of *genre*. But the form of the text itself is not, of
> course, identical with its *genre*: it is, rather, a unique produc-
> tion of it. (p. 85)

Many of Eagleton's suggestive analogies already contain the assumption that ideology is the source of literary form. The relation between literary text and dramatic production is compared with that between ideology and text. He wards off an incipient reductiveness by insisting, rightly, on the *internal* articulation of the text and ideology. The text is not a reflection of an extrinsic ideology but produces *its own* ideology which bears a variable relationship to 'general' ideology. Different works may be situated in the same ideological terrain but bear different relationships to it which 'produce' different textual ideologies.

One can readily agree that it is theoretically unsatisfactory to place art uneasily in limbo between ideology and science. But the neatness with which Eagleton reinserts art into an ideological domain is no less disturbing. Althusser's insistence on the category of 'real' art (one might prefer 'innovative') is based on the cognitive claim for such art which Eagleton's theory implicitly refuses. Unless we accept the notion that ideology can know itself, we cannot regard literature as essentially ideology (at whatever remove) without denying it the power to enact and discover to us the lineaments of the ideology from which it emerges.

French structuralism has without doubt succeeded in radically destabilising the concept of meaning. However, insistence on the *textuality* of all sign systems has obscured some important distinctions. If we examine the differences between literary texts and ideologies, for example, we notice that an ideology differs in having no specifically textual form: its discursive elements and themes are articulated in an imaginary space. Those texts which purport to transcribe an ideology are peculiarly vulnerable to ridicule and rebuttal. The strength of ideology lies in its *implicit* unity, which is dispelled when it is given textual form. The language of Freud's *The Interpretation of Dreams* is especially appropriate in the analysis of ideology. Like dreams, ideology has none of the specific textuality of literary discourse. The condensation of elements in a dream have imaginary unity and unconscious naturalness which conceals contradiction and displacement. The dreamer's report of the dream *is* a text, and possesses that specificity and materiality which admits analysis in terms of textual signifiers. The unity of literary texts is *produced* in the labour of writing and is not simply the effect of 'desire'. The unity of literary texts is no less illusory, but is quite differently situated. First, literary texts, especially the most innovative, lack the specious unity of ideology, and secondly, they produce a space in which ideological elements collide in uneven and unresolvable conflict, contradiction and difference.

Ernesto Laclau's *Politics and Ideology in Marxist Theory* (1977) has a special relevance to problems about literature and ideology, even though it is not directly concerned with literature. Laclau rightly saw that Althusser's rather functionalist theory of the 'interpellation of the subject' calls for revision. Althusser's account seems to require that all ideology must be dominant and can never fail to 'interpellate' individuals into their ideological places and thus to reproduce the existing social relations (Silverman and Torode, pp. 21–37, offer a more Derridean critique). Laclau, borrowing certain key Lacanian concepts (already used by Althusser in other contexts), shows that ideological discourses achieve a unity by 'condensing' various inter-pellations (political, economic, familial, religious, and so on). The unity of an ideological discourse consists not of the logical consist-ency of the various interpellations and elements, but rather of the ability of one element to *stand for* others within the discourse. One interpellation can evoke or connote another, even though they are inconsistent. The various elements of ideological discourse (national-ism, authoritarianism, militarism, and so on) have no specific 'class-belonging', and therefore may be articulated into any concrete discourse. This allows for the ideology of a dominated group or class to become a successful revolutionary discourse. A revolutionary ideology disarticulates the unity of the dominant ideology by insisting on the primacy of a particular interpellation, which then reorganises all the other interpellations into a new unity (by condensation). A recent example was the forging of a new dominant ideology in the Iranian revolution, when a religious interpellation became the catalyst in the process of disarticulating an existing hegemonic ideology.

What relevance does this have for literature? Literary discourse, it seems, has neither the 'unity' of a dominant ideology, nor the ability to disarticulate another discourse in the manner of a revolutionary ideology. If this needs qualifying, it is perhaps just to add that, if a text does possess the factitious unity or the simplifying reductiveness of an ideology, we usually dismiss it as propaganda or dogma. It is also true that literary texts often 'replay' ideological conflicts and attempt to impose solutions derived from particular class positions.

However, interpellations are effected much less easily in fictional than in ideological discourses. Therborn rightly insists that 'the rarest form of interpellation is the one implicit in the traditional historiography of ideas, namely, an elaborate written text speaking directly to a solitary reader' (p. 77). Innovative texts disconnect to some extent the elements of ideologies, not by effecting a reorganisation of a discourse but by dissolving its imaginary unity. This is not to say that literary texts may not have ideological effects or be appropriated by readers to the service of specific ideologies. It is to say, rather, that literature tends to *interfere* in the process of interpellation. *King Lear*, for example, allows the collision and disarray of ideological materials. The economic, social and religious interpellations possess none of the overlapping and mutually reinforcing relationship to be found in ideological discourse. The multiple and contradictory interpretations of the play partly reflect this difference from ideology. When literature veers towards propaganda or dogma, the effect of interpellation is simpler: its work ('hailing' individuals as ideological subjects) is either effected with ease, or positively repelled. Innovative texts have a much less definable relationship with ideology (though not an indeterminate one). It is this *difference* from ideology which justifies the concept of relative autonomy.

If we accept the theory of relative autonomy, we then require more than a general (synchronic) theory of the relationship between literature and ideology; we also need to produce a knowledge of the (diachronic) evolution of literature's inventory of formal possibilities *as they became foregrounded* in particular historical conjunctures. It may seem surprising to call in aid T. S. Eliot's essay, 'Tradition and the Individual Talent'. John Oakley long ago convinced me that the idealist materials from which the theory was produced do not stand in the way of a genuinely materialist appropriation of Eliot's theory. It is true that his belief in the presence of the past and the need for a writer to feel that 'the whole of the literature of Europe from Homer and within it the literature of his own country has a simultaneous existence and composes a simultaneous order' (Eliot, p. 14) smacks of the ahistorical idealism of his mentor F. H. Bradley. It is also true that, in his critical practice, the order of emerging literary moments of innovation does not represent 'the whole of the literature of Europe': like Arnold and Leavis, Eliot is always inclined to promote a selective tradition. Nevertheless, the central formulation of the theory opens the possibility of defining an evolving system and of satisfying both synchronic and diachronic requirements:

> No poet, no artist of any art, has his complete meaning alone. His significance, his appreciation is the appreciation of his relation to the dead poets and artists. You cannot value him alone; you must set him, for contrast and comparison, among the dead. I mean this as a principle of aesthetic, not merely historical, criticism. The necessity that he shall conform, that he shall cohere, is not one-sided; what happens when a new work of art is created is something that happens simultaneously to all the works of art which preceded it. The existing monuments form an ideal order among themselves, which is modified by the introduction of the new (the really new) work of art among them. The existing order is complete before the new work arrives; for order to persist after the supervention of novelty, the *whole* existing order must be, if ever so slightly, altered; and so the relations, proportions and values of each work of art toward the whole are readjusted; and this is conformity between the old and the new. (Eliot, p. 15)

F. H. Bradley's theory of Internal Relations provided Eliot with a powerful critical concept: on one hand, a fictional world is posited (the total order of literature viewed simultaneously); on the other hand, individual innovation on the level of practice both conforms to and modifies the 'ideal order'. The fact–value dichotomy is overcome at a stroke. The role of value judgement is clearly implied: 'I mean this as a principle of aesthetic . . . criticism.' Evaluation is not the imposition of absolute standards, nor is it the expression of subjective impulses, but is the practice involved in the dialectical restructuring of tradition in the face of the 'new (the really new) work of art'. Evaluation is the tracing or marking out of the key innovative texts or stylistic modes.

The Formalist concept of the 'shifting dominant', in helping us to theorise the appropriation of 'non-literary' forms of discourse into 'literary' discourse, also warns us against a reified view of literature as an autonomous region within ideology. However, this does not mean that we must accept a total relativisation of literary value. It is tempting to argue that any 'tradition' must be a selective tradition.

Raymond Williams gave us the classic formulation of this view: 'The traditional culture of a society will always tend to correspond to its *contemporary* system of interests and values, for it is not an absolute body of work but a continual selection and interpretation' (1961, p. 68). Tony Bennett adopts a similar position in *Formalism and Marxism* (1979) when he argues forcefully against any historical category of the intrinsically 'literary' and recommends a programme of properly historical study: 'The way in which the literary text is appropriated is determined not only by the operations of criticism upon it but also, and more radically, by the whole material, institutional, political and ideological context within which those operations are set.' (p. 135) On this view, no text has an objective value within the literary system; its value will depend on the context in which value judgements are made. To put it simply, this view regards criticism as a mode of *consumption* and not (even potentially) a form of knowledge; criticism must always discover an ideological value in the tradition it fosters, but cannot discover an extension of or innovation in the literary system.

I am arguing that a knowledge of literary production is possible, but I recognise that the history of criticism is hardly encouraging. Literary critics have usually engaged in various kinds of ideological or tendentious value judgement. One kind of criticism disguises a rhetorical preference as a commitment to some type of purification or elevation of style; 'simplicity', 'common language', 'nobility of style', 'naturalness', 'wit' have been some of the alibis. Another kind of criticism works by regarding one side of a conceptual or formal dichotomy as more healthy, or in some way more essentially literary. Such dichotomies include reason–feeling, organic–mechanical, prosaic–poetic, concrete–abstract, metaphor–metonymy, multivalent–univocal, realism–romanticism, realism–naturalism. Selective traditions may be constructed from these or other more ideologically explicit distinctions (high–low culture, ancient–modern, bourgeois–avant-garde). Individual writers may be appropriated selectively even though there is general agreement on their inclusion in the literary canon. Milton is a striking example of a writer who has been excluded (by Leavis and Eliot), or appropriated into various differently structured selective traditions. Could there be a criticism which stands apart from ideology?

Derridean deconstruction takes apart the hierarchical oppositions

upon which critical theories and practices are constructed, leaving no
ground for any theory to stand upon, including its own. History is 'le
text general', which has no determinate structure: 'We are always
engaged in interpreting this general text, making determinations of
meaning and halting, for practical reasons, the investigation and
redescription of context.' (Culler, 1983, p. 130) According to
Jonathan Culler we may try to justify our theoretical endeavours by
calling them 'language games' which are self-justifying forms of
discourse requiring no transcendent justification or grounds of
existence (ibid., p. 130). We are, it seems, compelled to accept either
that there is no ground upon which to stand, or that language games
are self-sustaining. However, Althusser's reformulation of a Marxist
theory of history assumes neither univocal meaning nor a centred
structure of determinacy, nor accepts the absolute autonomy of
particular levels and discourses. What kind of history does this
permit?

The construction of 'tradition' would not be an attempt to arrive at
definitive *interpretations* of specific texts, but rather would aim to
produce a history of the major redeployments of literary space,
which constitute a synchronic system in the present. This order of
the literary/fictive is dialectically placed in relation to and within a
larger history of the social formation as a whole. The history of such
a decentred totality will give us a substantial account of individual
texts' *conditions of production*. Far from providing a definitive interpretation of texts, this history will outline the structure of determinations which is necessarily decentred, contradictory and therefore *plural*. The *reception* of texts, therefore, must also be plural,
reflecting the various ways in which the elements of a historical conjuncture may be related, selected or suppressed.

The heterogeneity of responses to particular texts is, then, related
to the multivalence of texts. However, this multivalence is not a pure
openness or endless plurality, but a determinate plurality, reflecting
the decentred structure of texts. While I am proposing a history of
the literary system, I am also suggesting that specific sets of
(possibly) contradictory or unevenly related elements, constituting
historical conjunctures, do not allow univocal interpretations of
texts. We can, however, as I shall argue later, distinguish between
kinds of interpretation according to the degree to which they are
derived from the elements of a conjuncture or *forced* upon the text by

institutional, political or ideological determinants not belonging to the specific conjuncture in question.

From the point of view of deconstructive criticism, my project will collapse at the first hurdle, because once we deconstruct the distinction between the literary and the non-literary, which permits various hierarchies (philosophy is serious, literature non-serious, for example), we are left with a general literarity or textuality rather than a distinctively ordered realm of discourse. From this point of view, the 'literary' would embrace all modes of discourse:

> We think we know what literature is but are always finding other elements in it, and it expands to include them; there is nothing so definitively unliterary that it may not turn up in a book of poems. . . . The essence of literature is to have no essence, to be protean, undefinable, to encompass whatever might be situated outside it. (Culler, 1983, p. 182)

This deconstruction is oddly reminiscent of the Formalist account of literary evolution. While Culler concludes that literature has no 'essence', I would argue that the essence of the literary system lies in its ability to incorporate what is 'outside'. The Formalist concept of 'foregrounding' is a way of theorising this process of incorporation and of preserving the concept of literature.

The encounter between Marxism and Formalism in the 1920s briefly disclosed a theoretical space in which solutions to certain problems of cultural history seemed to be crystallising. Problems about the nature of artistic production, the relation between evolution and system, and the articulation of literary and extra-literary series, were being posed in a manner which avoided theoretical pluralism, syncretism and pragmatism. The Jakobson–Tynyanov theses insisted that the evolution of the literary system is itself a system. Such a view attributes structural significance to those moments which constitute the system's evolution – that is, the innovations in the system. A theory of the literary system, thus conceived, will attempt to assemble a synchronic corpus of concepts capable of articulating the structure of literary space, and will disclose the diachronic ordering of the system in terms of those innovating moments when the possibilities within the system were renewed. The notion of literary production inherent in this idea of system is saved from the one-sidedness of Shklovsky's Formalism by the concept of 'dynamic integration' which permits the theorising of the relations between adjacent systems, and by the establishing of a totalising problematic (the system of systems) which requires the theorising of the determinations of the specific systems in relation to the system as a whole (as in Althusser's 'social formation as a whole'). Thus the production of new possibilities in the literary system is intimately bound up with the 'integration' of extra-literary materials and with the structural determination of the system of systems. A full elaboration of the literary system, understood in this way, would require a massive labour beyond the scope of a single volume. In the next chapter I will attempt to examine the implications of the approach I have been outlining for textual meaning, and will consider specific examples.

5

The Plural Text and History

Degas's 'A Woman Ironing' (1874, Metropolitan Museum of Art) is open to several interpretations. We may choose to read the painting as a work of social realism, as naturalism or as a study in form. We may regard Degas as a Daumier, carrying on the class struggle in paint, or as a Zola, rendering actuality with a scientific precision, or as a Flaubert, performing a stylistic transformation of the real. If we consider the painting outside its historical context, it is evident that one reading has no greater validity than another. The 'text' remains an enigma, a hieroglyph, capable of reinscription in various ways. Evidently, the play of meaning can be set in motion in various directions, by the superimposition of various metalanguages (psychoanalytic, economic, moral, formalistic, scientific, for example). If, alternatively, we insist on establishing a historical conjuncture, are we thereby compelled to seek out a single 'meaning', the 'truth' of the work?

The historical critic is not forced to choose univocal rather than plural readings. To return to Degas's painting, there are a number of determinate elements in the historical situation of Degas's work which are not reducible to a centred, final meaning, but rather constitute a decentred structure, which we may call the work's *conditions of production*. This is not at all the same thing as a 'context' or a statically conceived background of historical ideas and events, which a work either exemplifies or transcends. A work's conditions of production determine the limits of its possibilities in certain respects, and provide the materials from which it is produced and which it transforms.

There is space here only to consider one aspect of Degas's painting. As Theodore Reff has pointed out, there are strong con- nections between Degas and Zola. Zola's *The Dram-Shop* began to

appear in serial form in April 1876 at about the time of the exhibition
in which Degas's painting appeared. The novel's protagonist is a
laundress and it contains descriptions of her shop which resemble
the painting fairly closely. Both artists concerned themselves with
naturalistic fidelity and trained themselves in the technical details of
the various milieux of ordinary life they depicted. However Reff,
discussing their interest in milliners' shops, comments, 'The writer,
it is true, was intent on gaining an encyclopaedic knowledge of the
commercial operation of such a store, whereas the artist, when asked
what he found so interesting in such a shop, replied "The red hands
of the little girl holding the pins".' (Reff, p. 168) Degas's interest in
the formal aspect of potentially tendentious subjects is often
apparent in his work. When he praised Daumier and placed him
alongside Ingres and Delacroix, his admiration was for Daumier's
draughtsmanship not his political satire. According to Georges
Rivière, 'Degas was more attached to the Goncourts than to Emile
Zola; their elegant realism suited the spirit of this well-born
bourgeois. . . . The painter professes the same disdain as the
novelists for people of a different social class than his own.' (Reff,
p. 170) Barthes emphasised, in *Writing Degree Zero*, that the
conjuncture of naturalism was the onset of modern capitalism and a
crisis of bourgeois ideology which could no longer make the world in
its own image. In this crisis, he argues, writing became problematic
in a revolutionary way:

> no mode of writing was more artificial than that which set out
> to give the most accurate description of Nature. This is no
> mere stylistic failure but one of theory as well: there is, in the
> Naturalist aesthetic, a convention of the real, just as there is a
> fabrication in its writing. The paradox is that the abasement of
> subjects has not in the least entailed the unobtrusiveness of
> form. (Barthes, 1967, p. 73)

In the work of Degas and Huysmans, there is a pull towards the
artificial even in the very moment of their insistence on the naturalistic. This paradox is evidently related to the question of ideological
crisis. Reff points out that brothels 'had a special fascination for both
Degas and Huysmans as a subject imbued with the melancholy spirit
of isolation and disillusionment which each of them identified with a

modern sensibility' (Reff, p. 80). A certain etiolation of art coincides with this disintegration of the heroic period of bourgeois culture. Valéry's linking of Degas and Mallarmé insists on the purity of this formal preoccupation: 'Degas saying that drawing was *a way of seeing form*, Mallarmé teaching that *poetry is made with words*, were summing up, each for his own craft, a fundamental truth' (Valéry, pp. 62-3). Jean Bouret places an interesting psychological construction on another of Degas's paintings of ironing ('Les Repasseuses', Louvre). He describes the vulgarity of the yawning woman and adds: 'But these details are forgotten in the charming colour-scheme; Degas ends by using colour to disguise the harsh impressions he had felt at the outset.' (Bouret, p. 164)

We have been sketching in some of the conjunctural aspects of Degas's painting in terms of socio-economic, ideological and formal levels. Certain contradictions (between mimetic and formal values, and between scientific and subjective values) are not simply arbitrary, ahistorical dichotomies which may be imposed at will by critics; they are distinctions inscribed within the historical conjuncture, which make up the work's conditions of production. From this perspective, if we examined the various actual and possible readings of the work, some would be derived to a greater extent than others from the determinate set of conditions of production; some would reinscribe the work's textual space in a more violently reductive way than others. It is evident that I assume the possibility of inscribing the historical field with a number of overlapping and yet conceptually autonomous discourses, where voices may be orchestrated in an often discordant but articulated totality. Without such a knowledge there is no reason to resist the urge to locate the reader at the centre of our literary theory (see Chapter 6).

We have already argued that, by regarding the literary system as a relatively autonomous instance within the total social order, we possess a model which allows us to develop a regional discipline of criticism without granting literature a privileged and protected status. Our discussion of Russian Formalism and T. S. Eliot pointed towards the development of a historical criticism capable of charting the 'imperialist' expansion of literary space. It may have occurred to some readers that the term 'intertextuality', familiar to French critics, is a more suitable one than Eliot's 'tradition' or Tynyanov's 'system' to denote such a discursive domain.

It is tempting to dismiss the awkward problems of structural causality and to capitulate to the charming goddess of intertextuality, in whose comforting embrace we may find an end to our troubles. In general, the term refers to a constitutive aspect of any text: namely, its repetition (that is, realisation, transformation or transgression) of other texts. By 'other texts' we may understand either the pre-existing literary system, or the total order of discourse, or the entire system of cultural (including non-verbal) codes. If we adopt the third conception of intertextuality (as understood by Kristeva), we would be in possession of a theory which embraces the text's relations not only with other verbal texts but also with other quite heterogeneous systems (including the system of 'desire'). Such an approach, for example, presupposes a knowledge of the relations between libidinal drives and the language process. The entire corpus of signifying practices is, in Kristeva's view, a vast text, a 'geno-text', which prescribes 'the possibilities of all languages of the past, present and future' which are subsequently 'masked or repressed in the pheno-text' (cit. Culler, 1975, pp. 246–7). History is thus cancelled at a stroke. Even the more strictly linguistic use of the idea of intertextuality tends inevitably to invite the semiotic sleight of hand, leaving the reader sleepwalking in a ghostly world of signs.

Even if one adopts a narrower, linguistic definition of intertextuality, the orientation remains ahistorical. The text's plurality is *underdetermined*: it is dissolved into an ocean of citations, echoes, clichés and undecidable differentiations. Laurent Jenny's development of a rhetoric of intertextuality helps us to understand the ways in which citations are absorbed in the process of writing, but he too opens up the prospect of endless semiotic play when he describes the reader's processing of intertextual references: 'One turns to the source text, carrying out a sort of intellectual anamnesis where the intertextual reference appears like a paradigmatic element that has been displaced, deriving from a forgotten structure.' (Jenny, p. 44) I wish to propose that we replace this timeless intertextuality with an intertextuality which, by searching for the text's conditions of production, redefines the text as an *overdetermined* structure. Charles Rycroft's definition of Freud's term is helpful: 'A symptom, dreamimage, or any other item of behaviour is said to be over-determined if it has more than one meaning or expresses drives and conflicts derived from more than one level or aspect of the personality.'

(Rycroft, p. 110) Althusser's use of the concept helps him to develop a strongly anti-Hegelian model of totality, in which heterogeneous systems preserve a relative autonomy but nevertheless form part of the social process. The text too is overdetermined in the sense that multiple and conflicting determinants are in play in its production. We are aiming at an intertextuality in which the play of meaning is held in check, allowing a plurality of voices to speak, in order to evoke a multiple structure of determinations and not simply to set in motion an endless semiosis. Eagleton's caustic remarks about American deconstructors seem quite justified from this perspective: they adopt 'the bare-faced device of transforming history itself to "text", sheer amorphous stuff awaiting the latest yarn-spinner' (Eagleton, 1981a, p. 57).

For Barthes, discourse is necessarily plural and may be forced into meaning only by an act of closure, an act which is the original sin in his theology. In the classic text, an 'illusion' of denotation is produced: signifier and signified appear to coalesce in an effect of pure reference, as a result of a *limitation* of the inherent productivity of language. Barthes demonstrates the illusory nature of 'realism' in *S/Z*, in which Balzac's apparently representational use of language is deconstructed and deconstructs itself in the play of codes. Barthes demonstrates that the classic text is susceptible of another, less reductive, reading, which is opened by the 'codes'. A 'limited plurality', which owes its readability to the work of 'connotation', is categorially distinguished from the plurality of the avant-garde text, in which the signifiers are given free play. Despite this acknowledgement of limited plurality, the classic text remains within the category of *écrivance* (an instrumental and 'innocent' writing) as distinct from *écriture* (a productive non-representational writing). Barthes's reading of *Sarrasine* goes against the grain; the promise of denotation hovers in the background ready to satisfy the reader with the finality of meaning. The classic text may be partially redeemed from closure, but only heretically.

It seems to me that we can no longer retain a view of the text as a centred structure, as a locus from which meaning radiates, but that the decentering of the text and the displacement of the subject as origin and source of meaning does not necessarily leave us with a chaotic field of arbitrarily conflicting or interweaving codes but with a more complexly structured discourse and a less unified concept of meaning. The critic is not restricted to the celebration of the text's openness, but can explore the multiple determinants which operate on texts at particular historical moments, both the moments of composition and the moments of reception.

This approach is inevitably opposed to several compellingly fashionable forms of relativist, sceptical and subjective approaches to critical reading. On the other hand, an 'allowance' for relativism may, it seems to me, be built into an otherwise optimistically cognitive approach. But an 'allowance' is not capitulation. Lawrence W. Hyman, for example, capitulates by neatly translating Barthes's indeterminacy into a generous and non-reductive form of reading which assumes a Keatsian 'openness' before the riches of the text. The notion of refusing to 'limit' meanings becomes a question of moral integrity and negative capability (Hyman). This approach offers no solutions to important questions about the production and reception of meanings.

In Barthes's usage, 'closure' is usually conceived as an ideological move, whether conscious or unconscious. The bourgeois novelist, in his view, restricts the plurality of the text in order to enforce the illusion of its naturalness, of its translucency. The world of the bourgeois novel has a compelling authenticity, probability and truth, all of which are a function of closure. Barthes disrupts the smooth linear surface of the novel by cutting the text into segments (lexias) which are then dissolved into the play of the 'codes' (systems of meaning); strands and streaks of meaning come into view only to vanish and to be displaced by others. Closure in the ideological sense is dissolved and demystified; each code calls up a voice, but the voices interweave in a potentially infinite polyphony (one might say cacophony). Thus, in Barthes's practice, the text's tendency to openness and indeterminacy is privileged. Liberty is preferred to authority. Unless we privilege some form of determinacy, even one based upon a plural text, we cannot avoid the scepticism which arises from Barthes's view of reading as an endless metonymic labour and of the text as 'an entrance into a network with a thousand entrances' (Barthes, 1975, p. 12). On the other hand, by adopting a view of the text as a determinate plurality, we may then attempt to ask questions about the total order of determinations which operate in the process of writing, and which we have called 'the conditions of production'. We must also be able to account for a text's reception.

A text is produced by the author working upon a body of materials (linguistic, ideological, social) which come preformed in some sense, before they are re-formed in writing. The conditions of a text's production include the following:

1 The Literary System. The conventions of literature include the constitutive elements of genre and the requirements of narrative. Meanings are produced by partial or total violations of conventions, but these effects are dependent on a sense of determinate possibilities of meaning. The conventions of mock-heroic satire, for example, derive from the violation of those of epic. Sterne's violations of narrative decorum defines certain effects in *Tristram Shandy*. The literary system is relatively autonomous (see Chapter 4).

2 'Intention' refers to the explicit marking out of meaning which consists in limiting the connotations which might potentially operate in the language for the 'ideal' reader of the period. In the 'Satyr against Mankind' Rochester reduces the connotations of 'right reason' by distinguishing it explicitly from a religious Neoplatonic sense. Pope's famous play on the word 'wit' in *An Essay on Criticism* operates within the context of the neo-classical formula: fancy + judgement = wit, where 'fancy' may also be called 'wit':

> Some, to whom Heav'n in Wit has been profuse,
> Want as much more, to turn it to its use; (81–2)

I am not suggesting that the meanings generated here are limited to those already inherent in earlier statements of neo-classical theory, but merely that in order to make meaning possible Pope is 'aiming towards' (intending) a verbal and conceptual space where significance has already been restricted. In Simon Gray's *Butley* (1971), Ben Butley conducts throughout the play a verbal rearguard action against the other characters who are in the process of abandoning him. His main weapon of attack is wordplay: he repeatedly deflects meanings perversely from their speaker's intention or fishes with words to catch out his victims. For example, he baits Joey's homosexual friend Reg with innuendos about homosexuality. Having succeeded in stinging

him with an equivocal use of 'queer', Ben reverses gear and makes
to cover his tracks by pretending that his usage was innocent and
at the same time apologising for it:

BEN: Sorry. It's an old nursery habit. One of our chars used to
say it. Whenever I came down with anything it would be,
'Our Ben's took queer again, poor little mite.'

Ben proceeds to ask Reg why he objects to the 'phrase':

REG: No, no, it doesn't matter. A misunderstanding. I'm sorry.
BEN: Oh, I *see*. *Queer!* – of course. Good God, you didn't think I'd
sink quite so low, did you?
REG: I'm sorry.
BEN: It's all right.

The effectiveness of the charade depends on the systematic
determinacy of the word-play. In contrast, one might argue that in
Finnegans Wake Joyce does not take aim at all or that he aims in
every direction. To use Anthony Burgess's words, 'the difficulty is
intentional'. In a later chapter I shall discuss the instability of this
'intention'.

3 Ideology, that common sense which tells us what the world is
'really' like, has a drastic effect of closure, and may be said to
operate as a horizon of meanings within which intentional
meanings may be staked out. However, once again, the effects of
ideology do not prevent new meanings from arising from the
production of the text. A work like Sir John Davies's *Orchestra*
illustrates a certain dominant Elizabethan ideology so usefully
because it produces few meanings beyond those prominently
defined in the ideology. On the other hand, Marvell's 'Horatian
Ode', although still written within an horizon of ideology,
produces new effects of meaning in its fusing of providential,
Hobbesian and loyalist elements. The effects produced have been
interpreted variously as Machiavellian, dialectical and neutralist,
but the possibilities of meaning arise from a determinate interplay
of ideological discourses, produced in a specific conjuncture (see
Selden, 1972).

4 Other historical determinants include the economic, political and

social. Just as ideology is a fundamental horizon for intentions, so the conditions at the level of economy and society represent an horizon within which ideology produces *its* effects.

Redefining the plural text in terms of a set of conditions leaves us with daunting problems of theory and practice, which cannot be adequately treated in this book. However, the example of Shakespeare's *King Lear* may provide useful lessons. Edward Bond's brief but suggestive comments on the play highlight the difficulty of making plausible connections between literary system, ideology, intention, and social and economic conditions. On the other hand his reading has a paradigmatic value from the point of view of any theory of structural determinations. Bond argues that there was a radical contradiction between Shakespeare's humanistic values and his own economic role. 'His behaviour as a property-owner', argues Bond, 'made him closer to Goneril than Lear.' When some important landowners wanted to enclose the common fields at Welcombe near Stratford, they approached Shakespeare and offered him a guarantee against the loss of the rents from the land (which formed a large part of his income) in exchange for his non-interference. 'Well, the town did write to him for help and he did nothing. The struggle is quite well documented and there's no record of opposition from Shakespeare.' (Bond, p. ix) Bond's reading of the play is derived from this context:

> Shakespeare created Lear, who is the most radical of all social critics. But Lear's insight is expressed as madness or hysteria. Why? I suppose partly because that was the only coherent way it could have been expressed at that time. Partly also because if you understand so much about suffering and violence, the partiality of authority, and the final innocence of all defence-. less things, *and yet* live in a time when you can do nothing about it – then you feel the suffering you describe, and your writing mimics that suffering. (Bond, p. vii)

It seems to me unlikely that Shakespeare was aware of any contradiction between his humanity and his own social and economic life, and therefore it is difficult to regard Lear as 'the most radical of all social critics'. He is so only if we perceive no contradictions within the play. The critical reception of the play makes it clear that totally contradictory readings are possible. Christian readings militate against nihilist readings. The storm scene has been variously interpreted as a purgatorial cleansing preceding a final moment of transcendent insight, as a vision of man's inhumanity to man, and as the ultimate statement of man's nothingness. The play evidently possesses a certain openness, and not merely a textual ambiguity. It presents a conflict between the values of charity and love, and of feudal responsibility, on the one hand, and, on the other, a militant individualism. The Christian connotations of the former are repressed, apparently in the face of the social tragedy which results from the unleashing of the violent individualism of Edmund, Goneril and Regan. The death of Cordelia and the absence of a reestablished 'order' at the end of the play do not restrict unduly the possible interpretive models one might bring to bear. The 'gaps' in the text may be filled in various ways. The Welcombe affair's relation to the play can be understood in the light of Althusser's principle of determination in the 'last instance'. The conflict arising from social and economic relations is the ultimate ground of the conflicts within the play, and yet no causal connection can be demonstrated (the hour of the last instance never comes), since the structure of determinations is *decentred*. That the play has been violently appropriated in one way or another by various readers is partly explained by the overdetermined nature of the text. Lear's speech on poverty ('Poor naked wretches') is susceptible of a more radical interpretation than Gloucester's ('Heavens, deal so still!'). We cannot close the gap between Lear's radical vision of injustice and Gloucester's more familiar Christian charity. This may suggest that Shakespeare has not resolved his thought, but it is more plausible to say that the conflict cannot be resolved formally within the play's economy, because the conditions of the play's production do not permit a seamless unity of discourse. Even if one chooses to regard the mixing of discourses as the effect of unconscious desire, this may be restated as the effect of contradictions within the ideological and socio-economic materials of the play.

While the determinate plurality of a text may give rise to contradictory readings, other readings may arise as the result of ignoring a text's historical conditions. Defoe's *Moll Flanders* was produced in what has been called, perhaps ironically, the heroic age of capitalism.

While Defoe's own mixed fortunes as an entrepreneur may lend Moll's ultimately successful enterprises the appearance of a wish-fulfilment, other meanings arise from the historically specific conflict between religious and secular discourses. The apparent incongruity between Puritan moralising and an entrepreneurial ethic appears less incongruous in view of Defoe's individualistic ideology. Max Weber argued that the religious individualism of Calvin produced a more starkly isolated inner self, and at the same time articulated the need, in view of the uncertainty of salvation, for a life of unremitting labour both in one's trade and in worship. Moll's deferred enjoyment of her ill-gotten gains and the careful garnering of her possessions are clearly in conformity with Weber's under-standing of the Puritan ethic. Of course, if a reader takes no account of the social and ideological discourses operating in the text, he or she may, and has, perceived irony in the novel or even satire. The plurality of possible interpretation does not invalidate the concept of a determinate set of conditions attending the production of the text. One may also argue that contradiction between religious and secular drives is heightened in Defoe's novel in a way which amounts to a critique of ideology.

It is not only readers in later periods who introduce alternative readings. Waller's *Instructions to a Painter* (1665) is a panegyric and heroic poem written within a neo-classical poetic and broadly Augustan 'common-sense' ideology. The poem's style permits only a secularised epic machinery and a peculiarly baroque grandeur, which creates a highly unstable effect bordering on the absurd. Sub-sequent satiric 'Instructions' (notably Marvell's *Last Instructions*, 1667) draw attention to this instability by burlesquing but hardly altering Waller's style. The instability of the neo-classical heroic is especially apparent in the heroic drama of this period. The dominant Augustan poetics close off some of the more ideal and escatological meanings of words like 'soul', 'love', 'glory' and 'mind', with the result that satiric and ironic meanings are produced involuntarily, so to speak, in the text.

Sometimes a literary work permits a wide range of interpretations which may be produced without departing from the text's conditions of production. One might say that the work's conjuncture is peculiarly productive of meanings. This is not to say that these texts are necessarily more valuable than other less plural texts. Gay's *The*

Beggar's Opera (1727) is a striking case. Not surprisingly, William Empson devoted a good deal of space to the play in *Some Versions of Pastoral*. In my view, Empson's brilliant proto-Barthian reading lacks a generative matrix, which would specify the text's conditions of production. From a post-structuralist point of view this lack is a virtue. I am inclined to think that Edward Wasiolek is partly right when he says that 'Empson was indefatigable in multiplying ambiguities and notoriously indifferent to contexts, a fact that is drawing some attention and admiration today from some structuralists.' (Wasiolek, p. 386)

At the level of literary tradition, Gay's essential contribution was the development of burlesque to the point of general subversion of conventional discourses. Vinton Dearing's remarks on Gay's early poem 'Wine' are relevant here:

> At first, he had a good deal of trouble in controlling the original elements in his work. In *Wine*, for example, he attempted too much: he tried to burlesque John Philips as well as Milton, the bathetic and the sublime at the same time, apparently with the intention of showing that all styles are contrived and perishable artifacts that need the poet's un-flagging devotion and application to be 'kept up', to use Keats's phrase. (Gay, *Poetry and Prose*, pp. 5-6)

This 'excess' is also apparent in *The Beggar's Opera*. However, I would interpret it not as evidence of a failure of artistic control (there may be something of this in 'Wine') but rather as an aspect of over-determination: disparate and contradictory determinants produced a strikingly fissured and relatively open text.

The multiple two-way ironies of the play are connected first with Gay's playing of one set of conventions against another. The burlesque of 'serious' forms is highly unstable: tragedy and farce, romance and satire, opera and burlesque of opera merge in perverse ambiguity. Gay's remark in the preface to *What d'ye Call It* seems to apply here: 'The whole Art of Tragi-Comi-Pastoral Farce lies in interweaving the several kinds of the Drama with each other, so that they cannot be distinguished or separated.' Gay undermines quite explicitly the neo-classical values of stylistic decorum which he apparently shared with his fellow Scribleran Alexander Pope who, in the *Dunciad*, satirised this very mixing of kinds in the work of the dunces. The beggar artist too resembles the indigent scribblers of Grub Street who people Pope's kingdom of dullness. Normally in burlesque and mock-heroic, the vulgar is ridiculed against a heroic standard, or the heroic is mocked and compared with the vulgar from an implied or stated standpoint of rationality.

Heroic tragedy, pastoral, popular ballads and sentimental comedy, in Ian Donaldson's words, 'merge bizarrely together, continually awakening ironical memories of other kinds of literary experience yet nevertheless forming a whole which is in some ways curiously life-like' (Donaldson, p. 163). The burlesquing of heroic or bourgeois modes has a less predictable and less orthodox effect than is usual. MacHeath is a genuine hero or honourable captain *and* an arrant coward, a romantic lover *and* anti-romantic rake. In Fielding's *Jonathan Wild* we never doubt Wild's villainy, while in *The Beggar's Opera* irony is unstable and sporadic. Polly's pathos and simplicity, and MacHeath's noble honesty as a highwayman coexist with unsentimental and anti-heroic moments.

This openness is unusually overdetermined. Like Degas's paintings, Gay's writings have a definite aesthetic detachment. He was fond of treating the mundane urban world with the refined brush strokes of Augustan style; the 'realism' of *Trivia* and *The Fan* is that of Lowry rather than a Dutch master. The familiar and the ordinary are worked into the charming frame of art:

> When dirty Waters from Balconies drop,
> And dextrous Damsels twirle the sprinkling Mop,
> And cleanse the spatter'd Sash, and scrub the Stairs;
> Know *Saturday's* conclusive Morn appears. (*Trivia*, Bk II, ll. 421–4)

The effect of such framing is, as James Sutherland put it, 'to soften and harmonize'; Gay did not emulate the naturalism of Defoe. Dr Johnson thought that *The Beggar's Opera* was 'plainly written to divert, without any moral purpose'. If Gay had worked to keep the play within the ambit of a moral theme, it would have had a less power-ful political effect. John Loftis's account of the various political appli-cations made by Walpole's enemies draws attention to the play's shifting identifications and multiple significances, which permitted an overlapping series of interpretations (Loftis, pp. 94–6). Gay's inversion of social hierarchy has the ambiguity of carnival. The play

is totally subversive and respects no one. Gay may be attacking the
rich and powerful, but there is no reason to believe that he favoured
social revolution (see Viner, pp. 92–3). In carnival, the order and
proportion of social hierarchy is thrown into disarray with a
remarkably unpredictable effect. As John Preston wrote, 'Gay
creates a . . . radical insecurity' (Preston, p. 271) in the audience.

The play represents the discourses of three social groups: the court
(aristocracy), the trading interest (bourgeosie), and the 'mob' (the
lower classes). The play's plurality of meanings stems partly from the
identification of beggars and thieves with both aristocracy and
bourgeoisie. Peachum, modelled on Jonathan Wild, the thief-taker,
is the embodiment of money values and bourgeois morality, while
MacHeath is the highwayman aristocrat, the man of nobility, who is
nevertheless inescapably enmeshed in the world of money values.

The identification of opposites, high and low, statesman and thief,
general and highwayman, is not new, but Gay produces it in a new
way at a specific historical moment. The celebrity of criminals (Wild
and Jack Sheppard) and the criminality of politicians (Walpole)
provided an unusually well-formed paradigm of irony. The comparison between Walpole and Wild was first made in 1726 by
Nathaniel Mist, the year after Wild's exposure and execution. In the
same year (1725) the Lord Chancellor was impeached for bribery
(Denning, p. 45). When the gang displays honour among thieves, we
note the absence of honour among the great men. When Twitcher
betrays MacHeath, we note the similarity between thief and great
man. The reversibility of thief/great man is an irony which is determined in part outside the play. This may *not* be true of the other
levels of anti-Walpole satire, which arise from the comparison
between the corrupt, vulgar, bourgeois Lockit and Peachum, and the
historical bourgeois merchants who were so deeply implicated in the
Walpole ministry's corruption, and aggressive commercialism. One
critic actually sees a sympathy for bourgeois values in the gang's
aspirations to respectability. Lillo's *The London Merchant* and
Steele's *The Conscious Lovers* both contain attempts to elevate the
bourgeois hero. Gay's echoes of Pierre's heroic ascent to the scaffold
in Otway's *Venice Preserved* probably confused a contemporary
audience familiar with Steele's new bourgeois ethos: 'Only three
years after the first performance of *The Beggar's Opera*, George
Lillo . . . was to imitate closely the final act of *Venice Preserved*. . . .

The fate of a London prentice, Lillo implies, should hold the same poignancy for us as the fate of Macbeth or Faustus or Pierre' (Donaldson, p. 164).

Gay's own insertion into the social structure was somewhat contradictory. He came from Barnstaple and his gentry family were involved in the West Indies trade. Having no independent means, he was apprenticed to a silk mercer in London until he launched himself on his literary career. His life was dominated by his relationship with aristocracy and by money. His writings abound with references to his financial problems; for example, 'A Panegyric Epistle to Mr. Thomas Snow' wryly jokes about the 'Millions of Imaginary Gold' which the South Sea Company's directors juggled with in the period 1720–1, when Gay himself suffered heavy financial losses on his speculative dealings.

One cannot say that Gay was anti-capitalist. His financial speculations seem to have been simply one available method of financing his precarious literary career. Nevertheless, there is probably some truth in Denning's view that the 'gang' in the play represents the ruthless world of business and finance. The poem addressed to the banker Snow, who did well from the chaotic dealings of 1721, is an amused account of both the poet's foolish gullibility and the banker's clever trickery. The imagery of the following passage captures the insubstantial and yet dangerous power of the money market:

> Why did '*Change-Alley* waste thy precious Hours,
> Among the Fools who gap'd for golden Show'rs?
> No wonder, if we found some *Poets* there,
> Who live on Fancy, and can feed on Air;
> No wonder, *they* were caught by *South-Sea* Schemes,
> Who ne'er enjoy'd a Guinea, but in Dreams;
> No wonder, *they* their Third Subscriptions sold,
> For Millions of imaginary Gold:
> No wonder, that *their* Fancies wild could frame
> Strange Reasons, that a Thing is still the same,
> Though chang'd throughout in Substance and in Name.
> But *you* (whose Judgment scorns Poetick Flights)
> With Contracts furnish Boys for Paper Kites. (17–29)

The self-mockery is balanced by a strong realisation of the cunning, invisible transformations of forms of stocks and shares which made

Snow his profits. The significance of Gay's complex attitude can be gauged if one compares it to George Lillo's in the Dedication to his *London Merchant* (1731), perhaps the first bourgeois tragedy, which was almost as popular as Gay's comedy. Lillo's dedicatee is Sir John Eyles, MP, who owed much of his success to his association with the South Sea Company, when he was appointed Sub-Governor in 1721 to assist in the reorganisation of its affairs. Lillo refers to this connection ten years later as evidence of his patron's worth:

> The proprietors in the South Sea Company, in which are included numbers of persons as considerable for their rank, fortune, and understanding as any in the kingdom, gave the greatest proof of their confidence in your capacity and probity when they chose you Sub-Governor of their company at a time when their affairs were in the utmost confusion and their properties in the greatest danger. (Lillo, p. 6)

Lillo's play is a celebration of Puritan morality and commercial ethics, while Gay's exposes the heartless individualism of modern society, as Lockit's soliloquy drives home: 'Lions, Wolves and Vultures don't live together in Herds, Droves or Flocks. Of all Animals of Prey, Man is the only sociable one. Every one of us preys upon his Neighbour, and yet we herd together.' (*Beggar's Opera*, II. ii. 4–7)

The other theme which runs through Gay's life was that of endless and largely fruitless pursuit of patronage, which was encouraged by his fellow Tories in the Scriblerus Club, a connection which inevitably brought him into conflict with the Walpole government. It is probable that, in 1727, he allowed himself to relax into subversiveness after he finally abandoned hopes for advancement, and burned his bridges by refusing the post of Gentleman Usher to the 2-year-old Princess Louisa (Noble, p. 5).

MacHeath's reprieve has several determinate meanings. At the intertextual level, the parody of operatic conventions is evident: a happy ending preferably with a *deus ex machina* was *de rigueur* in opera. The Beggar's final remarks point to another level of meaning: 'Had the play remained as I first intended, it would have carried a most excellent moral. 'Twould have been shown that the lower sort of people have their vices in a degree as well as the rich, and that they are punished for them.' (*Beggar's Opera*, II. xvi) Ironically, the rich are as villainous as the poor, but the poor are punished while the rich get off scot-free. A quite different light is cast on the reprieve, if we take into account Douglas Hay's evidence that despite an increasingly repressive state apparatus and especially the continual creation of new capital statutes, the number of executions for offences against property remained fairly stable in the eighteenth century. The Royal Pardon was more and more frequently used on the recommendation of the judges (Hay, p. 22). Frequent reprieves in the face of a terrifying criminal code legislated by a Parliament determined to preserve the rights of property would have produced a sense of the power of the law but also its arbitrariness. E. P. Thompson's *Whigs and Hunters* provides us with a detailed study of the Black Act of 1723 which, he argues, 'coincided with Walpole's final political ascendancy, and signalled the onset of the flood-tide of eighteenth-century retributive justice.' (E. P. Thompson, p. 23) That MacHeath is reprieved at the instigation of the Beggar has a further displacing effect: the unruly lower orders are made to mimic and thereby to subvert the authority of judges and royal pardons.

E. P. Thompson's arguments about the use of the term 'gang' are pertinent here. He shows that, while there were indeed criminal gangs (like Wild's), the widespread use of the term to describe all associations, unions, and so on, which were not countenanced by the law, gives it a distinctly ideological colouring (E. P. Thompson, pp. 191, 194). Gay appears to condone the ideology of the 'gang' in *The Beggar's Opera* (Denning, p. 45), but even this essentially conservative ideology is disrupted in the play of meaning generated by his analogies between Wild and Walpole and between criminals and bourgeoisie.

Several critics including Empson have noted the egalitarian quality of the play: 'Clearly it is important for a nation with a strong class system to have an art-form that not merely evades but breaks through it, that makes the classes feel part of a larger unity or simply at home with each other.' The Augustan view that men are all potentially rational becomes a more benevolent view of human nature in Gay and Fielding. But any 'levelling' tendency in Gay is contradicted by the gloom of the Tory satirists whose belief in man's actual irrationality lies at the centre of the Scriblerus Club's 'programme'. In the context of Walpole's depredations a certain gloom must qualify any carnivalistic or egalitarian response.

Faced with the task of summarising the meaning of the play, Empson can offer us only a list of 'a few approaches to its irony'. My argument is not that Empson produces too many ironies, but that he does not give us a sufficient sense of their possible contexts. It is not clear whether there are determinate conditions generating ironies and ambiguities or whether they are produced by Empson's reading methods which release connotations and plausibilities from the constraints of textual closure. When Peachum, in a double-edged moment of confession, says, 'In one respect indeed we may be reckoned dishonest, because, like great statesmen, we encourage those who betray their friends', Lockit, his fellow 'business associate', replies, 'Such language brother, anywhere else might turn to your prejudice. Learn to be more guarded, I beg you.' Empson's analysis of the double meaning is surely right: 'Either "it is not safe to accuse the great" or "it is bad for any man's credit to admit that in anything he is as bad as they are".' According to Empson, the basis of the effect is the fact that 'the primness of caution is merely indistinguishable from the primness of superior virtue' (p. 221). But this indistinguishability is not a transhistorical absolute but is made perceptible for the reader by the conditions of the text's production. The concepts of bourgeois virtue and 'great man' in 1727 both have sufficiently sharp boundaries of meaning to make Empson's ambiguity plausible.

The main theoretical argument which emerges from this example is in support of a concept of 'determinate indeterminacy'. This distinguishes the kind of historical criticism I am advocating from traditional 'background' studies and from textual 'interpretation'. The play's autonomy (its burlesquing of literary and non-literary discourses, and its aesthetic distancing of the mundane) is only relative. The interplay of meanings is both facilitated by and limited by the autobiographical, economic, political and ideological histories which, in an uneven and decentred way, form the work's conjuncture. Gay's own socio-economic position and the crisis of financial institutions in the 1720s give an unusually prominent role to Her Majesty the Economy, even though She can never expose her full power to the naked gaze of the reader. What if readers refuse to be historical critics? What if they prefer to read at will? It remains for the historical critic to elaborate a theory of reading which recognises this free activity – the consumption of texts.

6

The Reader and the Text

It is becoming apparent that modern Anglo-American literary criticism has been undergoing a paradigm shift since the late 1970s. The text-centred paradigm of New Criticism, explored and elaborated for three or four decades, is being replaced by a reader-oriented criticism. The shift cannot be located with the precision of an 'event' but a transition can be perceived clearly enough in the early 1970s (Slatoff, Fish, Riffaterre). According to Kuhn, 'normal science', the working out of a paradigm, occupies most scientists most of the time. The shift in criticism's 'paradigm' has been followed by a period of energetic critical activity, which has remapped the study of literature from this new point of view. It is probably premature, even ungentlemanly, to disparage the heir apparent to criticism's throne. After all, 'normal' criticism is looking for a successor to the jaded rule of New Criticism.

There is nothing new about a reader-oriented criticism (Tompkins, pp. 201–32). In classical criticism many of the central concepts (catharsis, decorum, the sublime) concern affect and reception. Renaissance and especially Augustan poetics promoted the social and ethical values of its aristocratic or genteel audience. The rise of aesthetics in the eighteenth century followed a general shift in philosophy towards a subjective focus upon perception (Hobbes and Locke), which was preserved and developed in Romantic criticism and the 'aesthetic movement'. Paradoxically, I. A. Richards, the precursor of New Criticism's text-centred approach, continued to examine, in his Benthamite fashion, the inner processes of reader response. The moral and social concerns of earlier poetics, and the psychological concerns of aesthetics inevitably banished the 'text' to the margins of attention. One might, therefore, regard the recent developments as the reworking of an ancient tradition. However, the followers of Heidegger, Freud and Saussure have produced new seams of phenomenological, psy-

choanalytic and semiological criticism which go beyond an exhausted
Romantic subjectivity. The editors of *The Reader in the Text*
(Suleiman and Crosman, 1980) claim a remarkably wide range of
adherents to reader-criticism. In her introductory essay Susan
Suleiman includes references to hermeneutics (positive and
negative), the affective stylistics of Stanley Fish, speech-act theory,
ego-psychology, the sociology of literature, Lacan's psychoanalysis,
Derrida's deconstructive criticism, Barthes's later reader-oriented
theories, and various kinds of subjective criticism derived from
phenomenology. These approaches transfer the critical focus from
the object of interpretation to the act of interpretation.

Reader-criticism has brought into question the theory and method
of New Criticism and other formalisms. To view the text as an
autonomous object, available for structural analysis, now appears
naïve. The dawn of meaning, hitherto the desired prize of critical
labour, has become a mirage. New Critics (with the exception of
Empson) ignored the fact of conflicting interpretations of individual
texts: they assumed the possibility of a 'correct' reading, or they
awaited the evolution of a more scientific criticism, which would
promote a consensus among critics. However, abandoning the
concept of determinate meaning may raise more problems than it
solves. The greatest shortcoming of reader-centred criticism lies in
its neglect of history. A text is produced within, and with reference
to, a conjuncture of historical forces. That is not to say that its
meaning is univocal, or that there is only one reading (reader), but
that texts are produced under a determinate set of conditions, which
may privilege certain readings at the expense of others. Reader-
criticism rarely takes account of the historical conditions of reading.

Several essays in the Suleiman and Crosman collection reflect the
influence of the later work of Roland Barthes in *S/Z* (1970) and *Le
Plaisir du texte* (1973). Cathleen Bauschatz makes an interesting but
not fully convincing attempt to interpret Montaigne as a proto-
Barthes, while Louis Marin's illuminating discussion of the narrative structure of Poussin's *The Arcadian Shepherds* concludes with a
total submission to 'the pleasure of the text': 'Demonstration or
fantasy, I leave my reading indeterminate ... my reading of *The
Arcadian Shepherds* has no other justification than my "delectation"
in a painting of Poussin.' Vicki Mistacco's excellent essay offers a
poetics of the *nouveau roman*; she recognises that to avoid all deter-

minacy in writing/reading involves transcending all conventions, categories and schemes. In the novel, this requires the deconstruction of all narrative and referential moves, a strategy for which Professor Mistacco adopts the term 'ludism':

> 'Ludism' may be simply defined as the open play of signifi-
> cation, as the free productive interaction of forms, of signifiers
> and signifieds, without regard for an original or an ultimate
> meaning. In literature, ludism signifies textual play; the text is
> viewed as a game affording both author and reader the
> possibility of producing endless meanings and relationships.
> (Suleiman and Crosman, p. 375 n.)

Alain Robbe-Grillet's *Topologie d'une cité fantome* (1976) is taken as exemplary: the novel instigates an unstable reading by continually sliding between categories. It occupies a 'tropological' space, and like Möbius strips and Klein bottles is non-orientable: both strip and bottle have no right-side-up or point of articulation; similarly, the novel cannot be oriented in terms of logic or representation. All identity is subjected to sliding (*glissement*). Pronouns are para-digmatic in this respect, and are used non-referentially to permit a random shifting of 'the situation of enunciation'. The philosophi-cal implications are summed up as follows:

> Robbe-Grillet intimates . . . a scriptorial/lectorial function that
> lies beyond the realm not only of individualization, but of all
> forms of exclusion and contradiction, a dynamic topology
> allowing sameness and difference, absence and presence, male
> and female, to connect nonhierarchically and without dialecti-
> cal resolution. (Suleiman and Crosman, p. 383)

Two questions arise from this radical deconstruction of reading/ writing. First, is it possible to avoid all determinacy? Can a reader's predisposition to 'normalise' the text be prevented? Secondly, should we regard 'ludism' as a method for reading all texts? The essay itself implies that there is a correct way to read the *nouveau roman*, but only in the sense that freedom is privileged and all conventions transcended. However, this is not the freedom of incoherence but a participation in 'discoherence' (the term is borrowed from Ricardou). The novel sets up its own conventions by proposing the transformation of a 'set of generators': 'Fluidity is a function of literary, cinematic, and artistic competence: the more one brings to the text, the richer one's perceptions of the generators will be and the greater the possibilities for play.' (p. 385; see also Eco, p. 40) The reader's knowledge of contemporary art, Robbe-Grillet's previous writings, and the history of poetry will facilitate this free play. The connections which might be made within this textual space are not determinate: 'no obstacle is posed to the reader's and the author's continued movement from text to text' (p. 385). It must be allowed, however, that while the connections made may be indeterminate, the references themselves are not (Mistacco names specific artists and poets). Does this not suggest that *at one level* a determinate reading of the text has taken place? Indeed, Mistacco identifies determinate features (shifting of enunciation, the liquidation of one set of generators by another) which enforce a labile reading and interrupt any attempt by the reader to construct narrative perspective. Despite her careful denial that the text is merely a parody of literary conventions or a subversion of the illusion of meaning, there are signs in Professor Mistacco's own terminology that 'ludism' is an impossible ideal. In the course of reading, 'generators' are 'liquidated', forms are 'eroded', and themes are 'deterritorialized or neutralized'. For 'ludism' to be more than merely subversive, it would have to achieve the normalisation of 'free play' and the eradication of privileged meaning.

The concept of 'free play' is linked with a strongly anti-authoritarian strain in reader-centred criticism. Mistacco talks of textual play in terms of 'an infinite, and therefore liberating, range' of possible meanings. Robert Crosman's essay makes explicit this ideological aspect of 'free-play'. He argues that E. D. Hirsch's assumption that a text has only one meaning is an expression of 'an ideology of society that is authoritarian and hierarchical' (Suleiman and Crosman, p. 163). Crosman speaks on behalf of 'mutual tolerance and respect for differences of opinion'. One can see how sweetly this liberating 'free play' harmonises with an Anglo-American free market economy! Some of Crosman's statements could easily be translated into directly economic terms: 'In order to serve the various needs and desires of various readers, texts *ought* to have plural meanings.' (p. 162) Of course, critical anti-authoritarianism has been more radical and even revolutionary (Julia Kristeva), but there are no signs of a neo-Maoist semiotics developing in the United States! A similar strain of ideological 'liberalism' is evident in work done under the influence of Derrida, for example in the *Oxford Literary Review* and in *Glyph*. Frank Lentricchia has wittily extended this perspective in his comment on American, and especially Yale, post-structuralism, which 'tends to be an activity of textual privatization, the critic's doomed attempt to retreat from a social landscape of fragmentation and alienation' (Lentricchia, p. 186). The ideology of 'free-play' has the effect of placing under suspicion all historical or contextual study. Historical knowledge as such is an authoritarian concept, it seems: we are permitted only to rewrite history *ad libitum*. As Lentricchia has shown, Derrida himself does not adopt such a naïve view of history. In the context of the 'melodramatic either/or' of the debate between the historical critics and the Derrideans, Derrida's work encourages no simple ahistorical hedonism, but recognises the 'ineffaceable historicity of discourse' (Lentricchia, p. 175).

Jonathan Culler has continued until recently (see Culler, 1983) to resist the magnetic pull of deconstruction, and contributed to the Suleiman and Crosman book an essay fully in accord with his important earlier *Structuralist Poetics* (1975). He begins by assuming that variety of interpretation is not a problem to be overcome but is the very fact to be explained by critical theory. He argues that, while critics may disagree about meaning, they follow a common set of interpretive conventions: 'A primary task of the study of reading is to describe the operations responsible for interpretations we find plausible.' (Suleiman and Crosman, p. 62) His first example is New Criticism's basic interpretive assumption of textual unity; readings may differ in content, but share this assumption. The susceptibility of texts to multiple readings derives from 'the potential reversibility of every figure. Any figure can be read referentially or rhetorically' (ibid., p. 65). The strength of Culler's approach lies in its promise of a genuine poetics, which would define the essential strategies of interpretation. Its weakness is the ahistorical view of reading which it entails. His excellent discussion of Blake's 'London' includes a subtle discussion of the lines

How the youthful Harlot's curse
Blasts the new-born Infant's tear
And blights with plagues the Marriage hearse.

After examining two political readings, Culler concludes: 'The accounts different readers offer of what is wrong with the social system will, of course, differ, but the formal interpretive operations that give them a structure to fill in seem very similar' (ibid., p. 64). A number of questions are raised by this. Are we content with a critical procedure which regards interpretive moves as material and the content of the moves as indifferent? Are there not historical grounds for regarding one reading as more pertinent than another? Will not our knowledge of Blake's other references to social repression make our reading more textually relevant? To re-use Culler's own word, which interpretations do we find 'plausible'? Readings of different degrees of plausibility may well share the same interpretive conventions. In setting himself a limited objective, Culler can claim to produce convincing results. However, his approach will not fulfil the task of determining the historical conditions of a text's production and the kinds of reading which can and have arisen on the basis of this history.

The leading exponent of *Rezeptionästhetik*, Hans Robert Jauss, in his important programmatic 'Literary History as a Challenge to Literary Theory', rejected a positivist historical scholarship in favour of a literary history which reconstructs 'the artistic standards of contemporary and succeeding readers, critics, and authors' (Jauss, p. 15). The only 'definable frame of reference' for a literary work is 'the reader's expectations'. A literary work may satisfy, surpass, disappoint or disprove the expectations of its first readers. Its initial reception establishes only 'the questions to which the text originally answered' (p. 23). We can never understand past questions except through the perspective of the present: the modern perspective of the historical critic has no privileged objectivity, but is a synthesising viewpoint:

> it is the successive development of the potential meaning which is present in a work and which is gradually realized in its historical reception by knowledgeable criticism. This judgement must, however, take place in contact with tradition and thus cause a controlled fusion of the horizons. (p. 25)

The problem with Jauss's position is that the relativism of 'horizons of expectation' is at odds with the aim of judgement and knowledge. The hermeneutic 'fusion of horizons' leaves the problem of knowledge unsolved. Jauss rightly emphasises the delays which may occur in the proper reception of particular works, and his analysis of the various possible patterns of reception is impressive. He rightly rejects an objectivity which seeks to isolate literary 'facts'; but he does not allow for the development of historical knowledge itself, only for a 'progressive understanding' over time. He recognises that the Russian Formalists' concept of 'literary evolution' goes beyond the limited objectivity of earlier literary history, but argues that their neglect of the history of a work's reception limits the validity of their formal account of its innovative features. It is true that a work's newness is not always perceptible in particular historical periods. While we must concede that blind spots in our perspective are inevitable, this does not invalidate attempts to map out the trans-forming and innovative moments in literary history. Jauss justly criticises the Russian Formalists for concerning themselves only with formal innovation and neglecting the content of form. Dis-cussing the social and moral effects of new forms, Jauss brings us back to the problem of historical conditions: the new narrative device in *Madame Bovary* jolts the reader 'out of the belief that his moral judgement is self-evident and re-opens the long-closed question of public morals' (Jauss, p. 40). If innovative form is capable of shatter-ing the reader's presuppositions in this way, then it should be possible to offer an explanation of this capacity which is not totally derived from our knowledge of a work's actual reception. The example of Flaubert raises questions about historical conjuncture (social conditions, climate of ideology, literary context, and so on) which Jauss's focus on reception at the expense of production prevents him from considering. Nevertheless, his work is persuasive in arguing the need for criticism to attend to the history of reception; any theory of literary meaning must surely be able to account for the variety of interpretations to which individual works give rise.

It is surprising that Jauss fails to recognise the possibility of *different* horizons of expectations coexisting among different publics in any one society (see Suleiman and Crosman, p. 37; Culler, 1981, p. 57). In the late seventeenth century, for example, different sets of literary and cultural criteria operated for the Puritan middle-class reader and the aristocratic wit (in this case, there was also open conflict between 'horizons'). Jacques Leenhardt's 'Toward a Sociology of Reading' also rejects the notion of the public as an undifferentiated whole in the discussion of readership. He describes an interesting piece of research conducted under his leadership at the Ecole Pratique in Paris: French and Hungarian readings of a French and a Hungarian novel were compared. A strong tendency to naturalise the alien text emerged: readers 'are . . . attracted to the stereotype that forms the basis of their reading; they take pleasure in recognizing themselves by recognizing their own mental categories' (Suleiman and Crosman, p. 217). However, because the mental structures of the reader do not totally coincide with 'the field of possibilities' opened up by the text, there is always the possibility of what Leenhardt calls 'short-circuiting', which results when a conflict of meanings cannot be resolved and the regulating system of the reader fails to master new material. Leenhardt considers that this effect of 'dysfunctioning' is peculiar to aesthetic works. By basing the research upon an extreme contrast of culture and ideology, he has made the theory rather less powerful; within a single culture one might expect naturalisation to occur more readily. However, there is no doubt that conflict of the stronger kind does occur within cultures, as in the seventeenth-century instance mentioned above. However, this example suggests that an ideological antagonism *within* a society is usually resistant to modification by short-circuiting: mutual stereotyping by Puritan and Cavalier makes satire, parody and invective the normal response to the alien text.

While it is true that the field of possibilities opened by a text may go beyond the mental categories of the reader, there seems no way of predicting a reader's way of dealing with the new. To go beyond Jonathan Culler's poetics of reading, beyond a theory of the trans-historical structure of interpretive moves, one needs to be able to establish a determinate set of historical generators of meaning. A literary work reworks certain specific biographical, intertextual, socio-economic and ideological (religious, political, aesthetic, and so on) 'materials'. One must also recognise that its reception cannot be contained within the space of this textual world. The reader may conduct the score in a wide variety of ways, ignoring some cues and exaggerating others. Reading may or may not modify his mental structures. One can talk of a text's power to modify a reader's perceptions, but, in actual cases, its reception will depend on the reader's own biographical, socio-economic and ideological position. This dynamic aspect of reception was well understood by the Prague Circle. Felix Vodička, for example, put it simply:

> As soon as the work is perceived on the basis of the integration into another context (a changed linguistic state of affairs, other literary requirements, a changed social structure, a new set of spiritual and practical values), then precisely those qualities of the work can be perceived as aesthetically effective which previously were not perceived as aesthetically effective. (Garvin, p. 79)

One must add that such differences in reception may occur within the same period and the same culture.

Consider two readings, by well-known critics, of George Eliot's *Felix Holt, the Radical*. F. R. Leavis's 1948 account interprets the characterisation of Felix as a failure resulting from George Eliot's lack of experience of working-class life and her over-idealising of the character: 'Felix is as noble and courageous in act as in ideal, and is wholly endorsed by his creator' (Leavis, 1948, p. 64). The characterisation, in his view, shows Eliot's intellectual powers and 'moral consciousness' failing to make good the lack of 'experience'. Raymond Williams, in 1958, found Felix an equally unsatisfactory character, lacking in reality. However, in his view, George Eliot shows a lack of *intellectual* power and moral feeling. He finds her understanding of the working classes full of 'petty cynicism' and Carlylean prejudice; Felix supposes that 'among every hundred men there will be thirty with "some soberness, some sense to choose", and seventy either drunk or "ignorant or mean or stupid".' (Williams, 1958, p. 116) Leavis and Williams ask similar questions, but arrive at quite different answers. How much significance should we give to the fact that Leavis was the son of a musical instrument maker in Cambridge, while Williams's father was a Welsh railway signalman; and that Leavis's anti-democratic élitism stemmed from a commitment to the 'petty-bourgeois' ideals of 'organic community' and the nostalgia for the life of village artisan, while Williams has adhered to socialist ideals of community throughout his career? I do not wish to suggest that their critical practice can be *reduced* to a reflection of class positions, but no theory of textual meaning is complete without including an account of the reader's historical situation.

This does not mean that only 'ideological' readings are possible. Leavis and Williams were directly involved in ideological struggle; this kind of 'moral' assessment of literary texts will always play a major part in the practice of reading. One Marxist tradition (which includes the later Raymond Williams) insists that interpretation is *always necessarily* engaged in ideological struggle. However, there is also a critical labour which is concerned not with the appropriation and subjugation of the text to a particular interest or value system, but with the delineation of its conditions of production and reception. In the absence of an account of a text's production we could not define the kinds of appropriation, negation, distortion or endorsement involved in various readings. Jonathan Culler distinguishes only between 'plausible' and 'implausible' readings. But who determines plausibility? The approach I am suggesting begins by proposing the need for a critical labour whose task is to produce the knowledge of a text's conditions of production. This knowledge will enable us to distinguish those readings which are produced from determinate historical conditions (biographical, intertextual, socioeconomic, ideological), and those which 'force' the text against the grain of history. This does not entail the assumption of a single correct meaning; Jauss is right to argue that a 'literary work is not an object which stands by itself and which offers the same face to each reader in each period. It is not a monument which reveals its timeless essence in a monologue.' (Jauss, p. 14) The knowledge being proposed is not of the text's meaning, but of the conditions of its meaning.

A simple example may help to clarify the issues. In Arnold Wesker's *Roots* (1959), while the family awaits the arrival of Beattie's boy-friend and mentor, Ronnie, there is a discussion about Stan Mann's widow, Mrs Mann, who had been forced to give up her job as a State Registered Nurse because she refused to stop 'living with' Stan. Jenny Beales comments, 'Bloody daft I reckon. What difference it make whether she married him or not.' (Wesker, p. 136) Jenny's attitude conforms to the generally lax sexual morality of the Norfolk rural labourers in the play. Stan himself, at 75, threatened playfully to have Beattie 'on a plate'. Jenny has an illegitimate child, Daphne, whom Jimmy Beales accepts as his without much fuss (he has not even asked who the father was). The prevailing attitude to sex is rather matter-of-fact and business-like. A London audience in 1959 would have seen the Norfolk attitude as unconventional, slightly shocking, and part of the low-life 'kitchen-sink' realism of the play. Wesker's 'Note to Actors and Producers' is carefully addressed to such a response: 'The picture I have drawn is a harsh one, yet my tone is not one of disgust' (p. 80). Many post-1968 readers will have a quite different response to the Bryants', Beales' and Manns' sexual laxity. This change in readers' sexual ideology and other accompanying ideological adjustments will encourage a reading of the play different from Wesker's 'intended' meaning. The shock effect of 'immorality' will be reduced or lost, so that Wesker's 'harshness' will also be mitigated. No longer will the exceptional vitality of Stan Mann be seen in its context of a dull routine of unconventionality. Of course, the changes I have referred to in social history are not absolute: different ideologies remain in competition after 1968. However, even a reader of 'conventional' views will no longer be able to respond to the Norfolk permissiveness as if changes in sexual mores had never occurred; their own moral ideas will be to some extent bracketed in a (perhaps only half-conscious) recognition of the changed society and the reduced power of their own predispositions.

To attempt to fuse the 'horizons of expectation' will not do. The changes in horizons between 1960 and 1980 will include the differences we have discussed, but the play is not merely a free-floating bundle of signs awaiting the shaping moments of succeeding horizons. The complex and historically specific conjuncture of Wesker's play included a dominant pattern of sexual mores to which the play 'alludes'. The Norfolk labourers in the play are marginal and 'backward'. Both of these qualities are partly connoted by their sexual unconventionality. It is evident that subsequent audiences and readers living a different sexual ideology may represent the Norfolk people to themselves differently, as merely slovenly, or as 'liberated', or as hypocritical. Such 'misreadings' are the inevitable reflexes of changed 'horizons'. However, such changes do not prevent us from distinguishing the historical material (the conjuncture) reworked in the play, even though this knowledge will not yield once and for all the text's meaning, since the text's discursive work does not end in a closed system of meaning.

This qualified indeterminacy and its effect on the reading process have been fully examined by Wolfgang Iser. The critic's task, in his view, is 'not to explain a work, but to reveal the conditions that bring about its various possible effects' (Iser, p. 18). Iser attributes to the text a certain activity: it 'interferes' with an existing 'world view', and presents the reader with certain 'response-inviting structures'. However, 'the relative indeterminacy of a text allows a spectrum of actualizations' (p. 24). Only the reader can resolve the contradictions between the 'perspectives' offered in the text. Indeed, Iser seems to have difficulty in resolving a basic contradiction in his thinking between the text's orchestration of the reader's response and the reader's 'composition' of the text. In so far as he presents us with a *phenomenology* of reading, his emphasis is upon the reader's unique appropriation of the text's structure of verbal effects. On the other hand, he often stresses the text's guiding hand:

> As the reader's wandering viewpoint travels between all these segments, its constant switching during the time flow of reading intertwines them, thus bringing forth a network of perspectives, within which each perspective opens a view not only of others, but also of the intended imaginary object. (Suleiman and Crosman, p. 113)

The reader moves from one explicit revelation of a perspective to another by crossing certain controlling gaps in the text. These 'structured blanks . . . stimulate the process of ideation to be performed by the reader *on terms set by the text*' (p. 112, my emphasis). The 'blanks' both invite *and* control the reader's activity: the reader does not merely internalise the various positions offered in the text, but makes 'them act upon and so transform each other' (p. 119). So, what is left unsaid at once determines the process of reading and leaves it free: the connections that are made by the reader will depend upon his or her own state of consciousness. This phenomenological aspect of Iser's argument installs the reader at the centre of the process of meaning's actualisation. The unexamined category of 'experience' shapes the process: the sequence of mental images offered by the text is translated into the reader's consciousness: 'The actual content of these mental images will be coloured by the reader's existing stock of experience' (Iser, p. 38). Iser omits consideration of the specific historical conditions of a reader's experiential schemas; he allows only for the difference between a contemporary reader's participation in a text's world-view and a modern reader's position as a detached observer of a past world-view. The failure to elaborate this side of his theory is inevitable, if Iser is to preserve the privileged category of the reader's 'stock of experience' (see Fokkema, p. 147).

The final appeal to 'experience' is unanswerable; that is its strength and its weakness. Despite his astute rejection of naïve substantialist conceptions of the 'subject', Iser's theory is founded upon a speculative theory of personality according to which the ego is able to adjust its experiential predispositions in an act of 'spontaneity', mobilised by the text, through which hitherto hidden layers of the subject's personality will be brought to light: 'The significance of the work, then, does not lie in the meaning sealed within the text, but in the fact that that meaning brings out what had previously been sealed within us' (Iser, p. 157). We undoubtedly need an adequate theory of subjectivity but surely not one that entails the endorsement of a transhistorical, reified individual. While Iser makes allowance for the historicity of world-views, his account remains schematic and disassociated from the social formations in which the world-views arise. His notion of a text's indeterminacy is concerned with the absence of explicit connections between its textual segments. He takes no account of the various kinds of extra-literary determinant which reduce textual indeterminacy. As I suggested in Chapter 5, our knowledge of Shakespeare's political and social outlook as expressed in his life and in his plays tends to discourage a naïvely egalitarian reading of Lear's 'Poor naked wretches' speech (though a 'forced' reading might insist on it), but not rule out the possibility of a 'crisis' in Shakespeare's ideology or a surpassing of the limits of ideology in some degree. Such questions go beyond the problems of the reading subject's growth in consciousness.

To grasp the historical grounding of a text's plurality, we need to understand the social and especially the ideological mediations of language. Literary indeterminacy, in my view, encourages us to make certain distinctions between literature and ideology. Ideology enters into the process of reading, but as a type of discourse it has a different relation to subjectivity.

During the last phase of Russian Formalism before the Stalinist period, the introduction of social and ideological questions into literary theory produced work of great value. V. N. Voloshinov, in *Marxism and the Philosophy of Language* (1930), attempted to find a way between an 'abstract objectivism' (Saussurean linguistics) which regards language as an autonomous system existing apart from actual speech or individual consciousness, and, on the other hand, the 'psychological' approach (the Vossler school which can conceive language only as 'the individual creative act of speech' (p. 51)). Voloshinov drew attention to the social and ideological mediations of language in actual utterances: 'Words are always filled with content and meaning drawn from behaviour or ideology.' (p. 70) He associated the view of language as objective system with what he called the 'isolated, finished monologic utterance' (p. 73). The monologic utterance asserts the authority of a single viewpoint and denies the complex, dialectical nature of human, social practices. In reality all utterances are essentially dialogic: an utterance is always either part of an immediate verbal interaction or is involved in a direct or indirect communication. Words are not fixed statically within an objective language system but are shifting semiotic material, whose significance arises as a communication between speakers in a social and historical context. This historical determinacy of the semiotic play is evidently difficult to theorise, but post-structuralists have over-reached themselves in assimilating the concept of 'dialogic' discourse (especially as developed by Bakhtin) to their own problematic.

Julia Kristeva showed correctly that Bakhtin's essential break with the Formalists lay in his rejection of their view of language. He went beyond them by developing a concept of 'discourse'. Language ceases to be the direct expression of a Cartesian ego, or the transparent representation of a 'reality' out there, and becomes the locus of a multiple 'I'. Bakhtin shows that Dostoevsky's novels are dialogic; no longer do we have a monologic world perceived from a single point of view nor do we have a multiplicity of views synthesised or harmonised by an authorial perspective. We have a dialogic world of unmerged consciousnesses. One might argue that Bakhtin here develops a compelling account of that 'impersonality' which T. S. Eliot found so hard to think in the unsatisfactory pre-Freudian language of psychology. However, Kristeva surely goes beyond Bakhtin, when she silently assimilates his argument to the structuralist 'disappearance of the author' (see Forgacs, pp. 165–6). Bakhtin always wrote of an authorial intention and an 'artistic will'. The abandonment of a mimetic or expressive view of language does not entail the 'death' of the author. In Bakhtin's and Voloshinov's formulations of 'dialogic' discourse, the plurality of texts is understood either as the result of an authorial strategy (some authors *are* monologic), or as the product of multiple social and ideological mediations. In these respects, these Russian writers remain on this side of the Derridean abyss (Silverman, pp. 305–14).

In Chapter 4 I suggested that Ernesto Laclau's development of Althusser's concept of ideology provides a theory of discourse which preserves historical mediations. Laclau's account avoids static conceptions of discourse and 'subject': ideology's 'interpellations' of individuals as subjects never form a rigid phalanx derived from a specific 'class-belonging'. The discourse of ideology is always liable to fractures, displacements, rearticulation and disarticulation. The position of the 'subject' is always under stress, even though complete disarticulation is rare. A dominant ideology is an ensemble, in which the various interpellations (religious, political, familial, sexual), even when highly inconsistent at a logical level, are mutually supporting, and form a condensation, which generates meaning and energy across the discursive field.

Literary texts, I suggest, may be inserted as elements in an ideological discourse (Orwell's novels are a striking example) or may be explicitly ideological. The following passage from Solzhenitsyn's *Cancer Ward* is an intervention aimed at disarticulating Soviet ideology:

> The Rusanovs loved the People, their great People. They served the People and were ready to give their lives for the People.

> But as the years went by they found themselves less and less able to tolerate actual human beings, those obstinate creatures who were always resistant, refusing to do what they were told, and, besides, demanding something for themselves. (Chapter 14)

The couple 'People/human beings' refuses the articulations of a

Soviet humanism, but noticeably conforms to a 'bourgeois' humanism. A reader may accept or reject the interpellation here initiated.

Catherine Belsey has usefully developed Barthes's distinction
between the 'classic' text and the plural 'modern' text. She adopts
Benveniste's term 'interrogative' to describe all literary discourse
(not necessarily modern) which has the effect of unfixing the
'subject', by refusing to 'close' the text's meaning in that seamless
unity of ideology. The classical text of 'realism' tries to evoke the
transparent unity of ideological discourse, but, as Macherey shows
us, even the most 'complete' work is necessarily incomplete, because
it has an 'unconscious'; indeed 'what is important in the work is
what it does not say' (Macherey, p. 87). In this sense *all texts are
'interrogative'*: they leave unfinished the interpellation of the reader
as subject. In Shakespeare's *Antony and Cleopatra* the Roman interpellations are organised by the political discourse, while the
Egyptian are organised by the private. Antony is torn between two
ideological systems, and his identity crisis remains in process
throughout the play. Any crisis in the audience's subjective identification may be resolved according to ideological predisposition. Even
in a text which has a relatively unified discourse, the reader may find
that the subject positions evoked do not form a unifiable ensemble.
In Dryden's *Absalom and Achitophel*, in which discourse is close to
ideology (see especially Schilling), the opening 'libertine' account of
Charles I's promiscuity cannot be articulated in a single discourse
with the 'Godlike' David's final apotheosis as saviour of the nation.
The subject position towards which the reader is being 'hailed' is not
'unified' as in ideology, but is specified in a contradictory fashion.
The gaps between interpellations interrupt the process of condensation, and therefore open spaces for readers to organise the process
themselves.

The reader's processing of the text, at this level, will usually
diminish collision and contradiction by organising the discourse in
response to a particular interpellation. In *Lear* the Stoic-Christian
interpellation (weak as it is in this play) is often the successful one. In
cases where an objectively weak interpellation is given a strong role
in the process of reading, we have what I call 'forced' reading. This
type of reading often moves in the direction of allegory. Where
readings of *Lear* involve the imposition of a weak religious interpellation, a full Christian discourse can be constructed (purgatory,

salvation, atonement, for example) and roles appropriate to the discourse given to the major characters (Edgar becomes a Christ figure, and so on). The medieval and Renaissance allegorising of classical texts is the exemplary case of 'forced' reading. Umberto Eco has argued that 'ideological biases' can work as 'code switchers, leading one to read a given text in the light of "aberrant" codes (where "aberrant" means only different from the ones invisaged by the sender)' (p. 22). He also argues that ideological biases are responsible for disclosing the ideological presuppositions of apparently 'innocent' texts. I would suggest that it is necessary to distinguish between these two kinds of reading: the former 'forced' reading is essentially ideological, while the second is much more critical and potentially cognitive. By distinguishing between 'forced' and 'derived' readings, I am not suggesting that the latter are correct, and the former false. All readings are misreadings in the sense that they must necessarily displace or supplement the text. However, the distinction helps to preserve the principle that the plurality of texts is historical and determinate. Whether or not the Christian Stoic interpellation in *Lear* is weak (or even absent) is not determined by the rhetorical strategies of discourse or by the slippery exigencies of signification, but rather by historical work, which may establish the play's conjuncture.

A theory of reception requires not a concept of normative interpretation, but of determinate conditions of production. It is not a matter of describing a spectrum of readings which approach or depart from a normative reading to a greater or lesser degree. Rather, a plurality of readings is what is to be explained (cf. Culler, 1981, p. 48). If the explanation is to avoid resort to conceptions of 'ideal' or transhistorical readers, we must assume the possibility of working towards a knowledge of the structure of determinants which constitute the limiting conditions of a text's production. If we do not assume this possibility, there is no reason to resist the arguments of Raymond Williams and Tony Bennett that, since interpretation cannot escape ideology, Marxist criticism must of necessity be 'partisan'. From a Marxist viewpoint, 'partisanship' in criticism has a vital role to play in ideological struggle, especially to recover subaltern and marginalised texts from the Lethean waters of historical silence. Rehabilitation of certain texts and the unmasking and demystification of others are characteristic practices of ideological struggle, but cannot be regarded as marking the limit of historical criticism.

Neo-Freudian French criticism has argued that meaning is always subverted by the perverse play of the unconscious which, in Lacan's view, may be identified with the play of the signifiers in discourse. We may accept that the unstable order of the sign prevents the final closure of meaning, and this always opens the possibility of transformation and violent deconstruction of discourse. Mark Cousins has eloquently expressed the daunting implications of deconstructive logic:

> Inscription cannot be held down, even buttoned down by categories of communication, meaning or intention, in such a way that those categories exhaust or fix inscription. . . . Any chain of written marks can be placed somewhere else, can be grafted onto something else. Writing is a spacing of differential marks: this is the condition of their being read. . . . But it is also the condition by which they can never be fixed, by which their repetition can never be limited to the 'realization' of an intention, thought, etc. (Cousins, pp. 72–3)

I would not wish to reassert fixity of meaning or to deny that writing may always be transposed and grafted. My argument is that 'history' is not reducible to textuality; that, when historical forces are transposed into the discourse of 'history', the forces remain as the 'grain' with which or against which the discourse pulls. It seems to me that it is the condition of all knowledges, including the natural sciences, to be always attempting to establish a new kind of adequacy in their discourses, not in terms of a progressive refinement, but by quantum leaps which are accompanied by changes in rhetorical strategy. Texts such as Derrida's *Glas* and Barthes's *S/Z* release themselves from the requirement of adequacy by embracing the fate of 'writing', which is to rewrite in the act of reading.

The aesthetics and poetics of reception have successfully challenged the New Critical credo of the autotelic text and of its essential meaning. However, the shift in focus from text to reader is the displacement of a partial truth by another partial truth. At its worst, the theory of reading descends to the level of Norman Holland's 'reading as a personal transaction'; at its best, in the work of Iser and Jauss, the constitutive role of the text is acknowledged, though it remains divorced from its historical conditions of production. If we begin by assuming that these conditions impose certain limits (or closures) upon textual meaning, excluding some significances, and opening others, encouraging certain ambiguities or ambivalences, and discouraging others, then we may be able to give a more elaborate account of the kinds of reading which arise. The theoretical distinction between 'derived' and 'forced' readings does not mean that a 'forced' reading is 'bad'. A derived reading may resemble a good translation, while a forced reading may resemble a good 'imitation'. The distinction marks a boundary between a reading made within the limits of a text's historical conditions of production, and a reading which surpasses, transgresses, distorts or displaces those limits.

My insistence on the concept of historical conditions of production is evidently vulnerable to attack by post-structuralists. On the one hand, they might (will) argue, I accept the plurality of the text (the play of signifiers), but, on the other, I preserve a totalising historical matrix (the signified). I would reply by insisting on the *decentred* character of this historical matrix: a text's conjuncture cannot cancel the play of signifiers but only mark out certain discursive defiles as the points of departure for subsequent readings. The readings will bear a *specific relation* to the text's historically inscribed signifiers even though the readings cannot be restrained in any way by these historical marks.

7

Literary Criticism and the Theory of the Subject

Persona, Implied Author and the Absent Subject

The term 'persona' or 'mask' has an almost *demodé* ring about it. Many literary critics regard the concept as either unnecessary (self-evident) or superseded. To write about it now is to disturb a grave, to rehabilitate a cliché. However, the dissemination of post-structuralist thought has had the effect of placing the old debate in a new light. The radical questioning of traditional Western concepts of 'presence', 'identity' and subjectivity, whether or not we agree with the new position, helps us to see more clearly the real issues which are at stake in this old controversy.

It is well known that the modern concept of 'persona' is substantially a revival of the ancient rhetorical notion of *ethos*. According to Aristotle the orator must create an ethical 'character' in order to make his arguments acceptable to his audience. The nobility of the 'character' assumed guarantees the speaker's credibility. In the absence of psychological concepts of 'ego' and individual self, the rhetorical distinction between the orator's character and the *ethos* of his speech raises no awkward questions about authenticity and sincerity. In the critical practice of the New Critics the concept became totally assimilated to *literary* 'speech' and acquired a more radical significance in its new context. The Kantian and Coleridgean filiation of the New Criticism stressed literature's special and even autonomous status. As a result, the voices and personae constructed by the author inevitably became distinguished more radically from the author's own personality. The distinctly subversive aspects of this separation, which went beyond a purely rhetorical position, were not made explicit nor were they even intended. Some of the New Critics drew upon the poetic practice and the marginal commentaries of Yeats, Eliot and Pound to strengthen the case for placing the 'author' in parentheses. The castigation of the biographical fallacy entailed the rejection of a simplistic identification of author and speaker. Literature's 'voices' were conceived as rhetorically constructed devices rather than immediately expressive utterances. However, it soon became apparent that the displacement of the author concealed the mechanism of a more radical impersonality. The hidden implication, which had already made its appearance in the poetry of Eliot and Yeats, remained hidden and even repressed, since to acknowledge that the author was not the parent of his voices would have undermined the fundamental humanist faith of the New Critic. Most critics in the 1950s and 1960s accepted the concept of persona but always upon the stated or unstated understanding that the author retained his status as an underlying 'presence' as creator and source of his voices. The challenge presented by the French post-structuralists, especially Lacan, Derrida and Kristeva, consists precisely in their abandonment of the philosophy of 'presence' for a theory which conceives the 'subject' as the site of a process of signification, and not a point of origin. From the point of view of the predominant literary humanism of Anglo-American criticism, the 'anti-humanism' of these writers is 'unthinkable'; the implications of such views are too radical for even a partial assimilation.

Persona

It is important to establish at the outset a tentative typology of the concept 'persona' in order to avoid unnecessary ambiguity. The primary dramatic metaphor of the mask establishes at once an *identity* and a *difference*. The voice projected from the mask is the *same* voice as the author's. But the projection also involves the objectification of *another* voice. The different interpretations of persona stem partly from the different emphases placed on sameness and difference. The former emphasis facilitates the closing of the distinction between author and persona, so that we are left with a *propria persona*. The emphasis on difference detaches the persona as a *dramatis persona*. The romantic poetry of Wordworth insists on the sole authenticity of the *propria persona*. Modernist poetry insists on the authenticity of the *dramatis persona*. In the former, the author's persona is a full presence, in the latter, the author is absent, a hidden god behind his personae.

Within these two broad categories some clear subcategories may be outlined. Augustan satirists do not speak strictly *in propria persona* but project personae which appear to emanate from a *propria persona*. William B. Ewald describes Swift's personae in these terms:

> The Jonathan Swift of the sermons is still Jonathan Swift when he writes indecent verses, even though his attitude is so different that he seems to be almost another person. To begin to understand the 'whole' man, one must recognise all his poses. (Ewald, pp. 10–11)

We are faced here with a fundamental problem: are we to regard the 'whole' man in materialist terms as the sum of his masks or in idealist terms as the spirit (or mind) which underlies (as an immanent cause) or transcends the masks? The problem usually remains unarticulated, but is probably the prime metaphysical obstacle to a solution of the general controversy.

Within the category of the *dramatis persona* a number of subcategories may be introduced, depending on the degree of the persona's apparent autonomy. In Restoration comedy, the normative point of view of an implied author is usually strongly indicated in the ordering of the relations between personae. We normally know where the author stands. Mikhail Bakhtin proposed the category of 'carnivalistic' literature, in which personae possess a radical autonomy: the points of view of 'unmerged consciousnesses' are not subordinated to a normative point of view, but enter into a dialectical relationship with the authorial voice. Presumably Browning's dramatic monologues belong to an intermediate class in which there is a split in the reader's response between 'sympathy' and 'judgement' (Langbaum, p. vii), that is between a 'carnivalistic' and a normative response. Alternatively, we may assimilate Browning to the first category by concluding with J. Hillis Miller that Browning's 'self-hood' is constituted by the enactment in imagination of the 'roles of the most diverse people' in an attempt to 'satisfy all the impulses of his being' (Miller, p. 105). Indeed the theory of the author/persona relationship is bedevilled by the fact that critics pass so easily from one side of the opposition to the other in their attempts to locate the object of their scrutiny. The classification sketched above may be summarised as follows:

1 *Propria Persona*
   (a) 'Direct' expression (Wordsworth).
   (b) 'Indirect' expression (Swift, Pope).
2 *Dramatis Persona*
   (a) Personae organised from a point of view (Restoration Comedy).
   (b) Personae relatively autonomous (Dostoevsky).

There is a strong tendency, which may be termed a 'humanist' tendency, among many critics to reduce the problem to one of *authenticity*. The very term 'persona' would to them imply inauthenticity, the playing of roles, the disguising or concealing of the 'inner self'. For them the romantic refusal of rhetoric is the ultimate moment of authenticity, when the inner self achieves a pure transparency of expression in a total 'presence'.

The 'humanist' tendency even survives, though less comfortably, in the more rhetorical approaches to the problem. Wayne Booth's important contribution to the theory of narrative turns upon the concept of the 'implied author'. Recognising that, in novels, the point of view emanating from the 'author' is not necessarily the same as a persona or a narrator, Booth introduces the term 'implied author', as distinct from 'real author', in order to describe the picture formed by the reader of the 'official scribe' or 'second self' who presides over the novel. Having made this important distinction between 'implied' and 'real' authors, he goes on to underline the fact that the implied author, far from being a neutral artistic device, is a real centre of moral norms. Far from involving a loss of authenticity, the artistic construction of implied authors provides the real authors with what may be their only real moments of 'sincerity':

> A great work establishes the 'sincerity' of its implied author, regardless of how grossly the man who created that author may belie in his *other* forms of conduct the values embodied in his work. For all we know, the only sincere moments of his life may have been lived as he wrote his novel. (Booth, p. 75)

Arnold Wesker's *Roots* concludes with Beattie's discovery of her own voice in a moment of ecstatic realisation:

> D'you hear that? D'you hear it? Did you listen to me? I'm
> talking. Jenny, Frankie, Mother – I'm not quoting no
> more.... Listen to me someone. As though a vision were
> revealed. God in heaven, Ronnie! It does work, it's happening
> to me, I can feel it's happened, I'm beginning, on my own two
> feet – I'm beginning. ...

Beattie, it seems, is about to lay aside a role she had been playing –
she is about to become herself. The change is signified by a change
from 'quoting' to authentic articulateness. (The concluding stage
direction tells us that Beattie 'stands alone, articulate at last'.) Beattie
signals her entry into authenticity of being by creating her own
metaphor – 'roots', where earlier she had quoted Ronnie's metaphor
(words are 'bridges'). The distinction is strangely formalistic and
unconvincing at the level of characterisation. Wesker cannot convey
the distinction between authentic and inauthentic speech except
through a formal linguistic sign. Beattie's personality and identity
are no less *there* in the earlier part of the play than in the revelatory
conclusion. It would be possible to accept that Beattie has become
more articulate at the end of the play, that she has learnt to use
Ronnie's language. But her last words 'I'm beginning' announce the
inauguration of an authentic self and not merely a verbal mastery.
Her quotations from Ronnie had signified her adoption of a mask, a
voice and language which she mimicked and which had no deeper
connection with her own personality. At the end of the play Beattie
speaks in *propria persona*. The mask and the face are one. But, if we
remove the quotation marks (in the text) and the constantive 'Ronnie
says' we are left with substantially the same voice. Is Ronnie still
speaking unacknowledged? Is Wesker speaking? Or is the text
speaking? A traditional humanist answer might suggest that Beattie's
revelation is an endorsement of Wesker's own faith in the possibility
of self-realisation through articulateness. A more radical answer
might suggest that the authentic self discovered by Beattie is a
mythic or ideological construct: the distinction between an inner self
and an outer self dissolves with the distinction between author and
mask.

Rhetoric and New Criticism

With the possible exception of Longinus classical poetics is dominated by rhetoric: it characteristically treats writing in forensic
terms. The poet is obliged to *convince* his reader; his own character
must appear good in order to give conviction to his words. Elder
Olson, the neo-Aristotelian critic, offers a rhetorical reading of
Pope's *Epistle to Dr. Arbuthnot* which closely touches on the problem of persona. Following the *Rhetoric* of Aristotle, Olson shows
that Pope's defence of his own character is a strictly rhetorical
achievement:

> One thing must be remarked at once: such questions as
> whether Pope's indignation is sincere, or whether Pope was
> actually a man of good character – questions about which his
> critics have troubled so much – are entirely irrelevant here.
> The rhetorician need not actually be sincere, need not actually
> be a good man; he must, however, *seem* to be these things, that
> is, he must through his art effect the impression that he is these
> things; it is far more important, from the standpoint of
> rhetoric, to seem to have good character when one actually
> does not, than to have it when one does not seem to. (Olson,
> pp. 39–40)

Olson adds that the appearance of virtue is enough for forensic
rhetoric but 'to judge the work as *demonstration* there would be re-
quisite a certitude, which no historical information could provide,
that Pope was in fact virtuous.' From this point of view there is an
unfathomable gap between author and persona. Objectively, the
voice of the text can only possess the semblance of authenticity. The
audience or reader may attribute authenticity to the author, but this
cannot be deduced from the text.

Pope's satires have long been the subject of controversy between
the proponents of biographical criticism and rhetorical criticism.
Maynard Mack argued that the critic must make a clear demarcation
between Pope and his persona. He attributed three voices to Pope's
persona: the plain-living, self-amused voice of the *vir bonus*, the
naïve voice of the *ingénu*, and the heroic voice of public defender

(Mack). Each voice represents a different ethical strategy, a means of directing satiric praise and blame through confession, irony or declamation. Mack's approach is typical of New Criticism's use of the concept of persona in so far as it entails a *bracketing* of the author, and a rather gestural assertion of the autonomy of literary texts. The resulting ambiguity surrounding the status of the author's relationship to his personae left a number of more traditional critics very uneasy.

Irving Ehrenpreis, in a celebrated essay, boldly attempted to reinstate the inner self at the centre of the text. He argued that the poses and roles which the self plays are not 'illusory appearances', but 'visible effluences, aspects, reflections – however indirect – of an inner being that cannot be defined apart from them.' (Ehrenpreis, p. 31) Such metaphysical confidence can hardly be shaken by argument. Ehrenpreis's essay reflects the firm faith of Western philosophy in the doctrine of total 'presence', and of semantic anthropocentrism. To accept the displacement of the author as immanent cause and as the centre of his play of voices would be equivalent to accepting a Copernican revolution in philosophy. The New Critics cannot be regarded as having inaugurated such a revolution. The rhetorical 'bracketing' of the author's own character leaves the 'inner being' intact as a putative 'presence'. For example, Wayne Booth, after exploring the full range of narrative voices and authorial strategies which make up the rhetoric of fiction, concluded his inventory with a chapter on the 'Morality of Narration', in which the author's moral responsibility for his voices is uncompromisingly asserted. Attacking Céline for not clearly ironising the nihilistic world-view of Bardamu in *Journey to the End of the Night*, he declares, 'Though Céline has attempted the traditional excuse – remember, it is my character speaking and not I – we cannot excuse him for writing a book which, if taken seriously by the reader, must corrupt him.' (Booth, p. 383) The author is the responsible source and regulator of his rhetorical progeny: he speaks of them. There are no gaps and no displacements in the signifying process when rhetorical theories are thus safeguarded. As Ehrenpreis puts it, 'only as a relationship between a real speaker and a real listener can meaning exist'. Ambiguities, uncertainties and polyvalencies in the ordering of fictional voices become aesthetic or moral lapses unless they can be reinstated as 'tensions' (that is, as the aesthetic forms of moral detachment). In retrospect it is clear that Ehrenpreis's fear of an anti-humanist tendency in the rhetorical criticism of Mack, Olson, Rebecca Parkin, George T. Wright and others was not well founded. The breach between author as man and author as poet was easily closed by various strategies whether psychological, mystical or formalistic. The symposium on 'The Concept of Persona in Satire', published in *Satire Newsletter*[1] is remarkable for its conciliatory response to Ehrenpreis's challenge. Most contributors thought that he had constructed a straw man in his image of the New Critic who insists as a matter of principle that 'a literary work should be regarded not as an aspect of the author's personality but as a separate thing'. W. S. Anderson concedes the argument immediately: 'Yet I believe that the satires do spring, *in some inexplicable way*, from Juvenal's personality' (p. 91, my emphasis). W. F. Cunningham makes a common-sense compromise: the satirist both 'structures an artifice' *and* 'offers a certain kind of self-revelation' (p. 94). The concept of persona is useful, argue several contributors, to denote those *partial revelations* of authorial character which are made in individual works. Rhetorical concepts help the critic to differentiate between authors' selective expressions of self.

While it may be true that most New Critics were anxious to temper the excesses of formalism and to preserve a romantic-humanist concept of the author, this cannot be said of all Anglo-American critics of the middle third of the century, especially those most deeply influenced by the modernist revolution associated with the poetry of Yeats, Eliot and Pound. The challenge to the humanist hegemony presented by the poetic *practice* of these writers went far beyond the theoretical response of most New Critics.

Eliot, Yeats and Pound

The deployment of masks or personae by Yeats, Eliot and Pound varies substantially, but in each case a decisive break with the romantic identification of poet and persona is made. The impersonality of Keats differs radically from Eliot's in this respect. The annihilation of the self in Keats is not the annihilation of the expressive self of the text but rather an empathic moment of identification of subject and object prior to composition. In Eliot impersonality permeates the 'voice' of the text. The polyphony of voices in *The Waste Land* reflects a consciousness but not a personality. George T. Wright has charted the transition from the romantic lyric, in which the experiencing poet/persona is the centre of the poem's communicative stream, to the modern lyric in which the persona is displaced as centre: 'In the poetic structure characteristically used by modernist poets at least, the self, though still (and presumably eternally) the observing instrument and even the scene of conflict, is no longer the center of significance' (Wright, p. 57). The work itself – the artistic labour – becomes the centre. Eliot's own thinking about the relationship between the poet's personality and his work is somewhat muddled and contradictory, but engages with a real theoretical problem. His critique of romanticism is forthright and unequivocal: 'Poetry is not a turning loose of emotion, but an escape from emotion; it is not the expression of personality, but an escape from personality.' Yet the poet's emotions are the starting-point of his work, which involves the 'transfusion of the personality' into 'something rich and strange, something universal and impersonal'. (Eliot, pp. 21, 137) Eliot's explicit philosophical reasoning underlines the radical nature of his view:

> The point of view which I am struggling to attack is perhaps related to the metaphysical theory of the substantial unity of the soul: for my meaning is, that the poet has, not a 'personality' to express, but a particular medium, which is only a medium and not a personality. (p. 20)

Elsewhere Eliot preserves the concept of personality to describe the distinctiveness of the tones which unify a work. Nevertheless, the idea of the self as a *locus*, as a space in which disparate 'feelings' may combine and recombine remains central. The self, in other words, is no longer an authentic source, a substantial presence, but the site of processes of structuration. The fictive personae are similarly decentred. Even Prufrock is a radically divided voice. An 'I' and the 'you' merge in a 'we'. The quotidian voice of Prufrock is invaded by other voices of the hero, the fool and the *id*. The unfashionable middle-aged 'I' strolling by the beach becomes the hidden 'we' buried beneath the human:

We have lingered in the chambers of the sea
By sea-girls wreathed with seaweed red and brown
Till human voices wake us, and we drown.

The poem silently speaks of that unconscious which had not long
been discovered by Freud. The idea of a divided self is not a twentieth-century idea. However the *structure* of the Freudian unconscious has a very specific relation to the structure of modernist
poetry and prose fiction. The processes of condensation and displacement which produce the structures of the dream-work are
closely related to the principles of structuration in a modernist poem.
Or rather, the modernist poem manifests a structure which, like the
structure of dream-work, may in fact be the latent structure of all art
and all language.

Oscar Wilde's perverse and witty inversion of nature's priority
over art entailed a similar valorising of the 'artificial' mask at the
expense of the 'natural' personality: 'Man is least himself when he
talks in his own person. Give him a mask and he will tell you the
truth.' (Wilde, p. 164) Yeats was profoundly attracted to Wilde's
aesthetic notions (Ellmann, 1967). Wilde's theory of masks reappears without modification in *Per Amica Silentia Lunae*, where
Yeats describes the personalities of St Francis and Caesar Borgia
as imitations of Christ and Caesar: they 'made themselves over-
mastering, creative persons by turning from the mirror to meditation
upon a mask'. Taking Wilde's amusing and subversive assertion as
his starting-point, Yeats undertook an exploration of the fictive mask
in its dialectical unfolding of the contradictory selves which constitute the contested site of the personality. Yeats goes beyond
Browning in recognising that not only the social self but also the
private self are 'masks'. The attainment of the sense of an authentic
self, of a spontaneous or instinctive mode of existence, was to him a
lost struggle: 'All my moral endeavour for many years has been an
attempt to recreate practical instinct in myself. I can only conceive of
it as of a kind of acting.' (Ellmann, 1961, p. 178) There is here a
romantic concern for the loss of spontaneity as a result of the domination of instinct by analytic reason. But whatever metaphysical
underpinning sustained Yeats's exploration of the masks of the self,
the poetic texts subvert unequivocally the concept of the substantial

self, of the point of origin, and thus call into question the imputed presence of the poet himself. The problem is usually solved by invoking the notion of the mask as an evasion or concealment, an unwillingness to expose or recognise the 'real' self. The same kind of rationalisation can be made in the case of Swift, Wilde, Wallace Stevens and Pound. Indeed, role-playing in general may be regarded either as the *concealment* of self or as the *discovery* of self. However, from a more radical point of view one might see role-playing either as existential project or as self-production.

Pound's reflections upon the disintegration of the self are the most radical in the modernist period. His well-known remarks of 1916 are very explicit:

> In the 'search for oneself' in the search for 'sincere self-expression', one gropes . . . for some seeming verity. One says 'I am' this, that or the other, and with the words scarcely uttered one ceases to be that thing. . . . I began this research for the real in a book called *Personae*, casting off, as it were, complete masks of the self in each poem. I continued in a long series of translations, which were but more elaborate masks. (Pound, 1916, p. 98)

For Pound the search is not a voyage of discovery, but the necessary search for congenial residences, for a 'true' homeland of the self. Pound's continuous engagement with the theory and practice of translation and imitation is the characteristic moment in his commitment to impersonality. In Pound the habitual self is not so much refined out of existence as called into question. Among the modernists, in Pound above all, the self is divided. In 'The Flame' Pound adopts the mask of a sublime bard whose Paterian ecstasy concludes in a remarkable and unPaterian dissolving of selfhood:

> If I have merged my soul, or utterly
> Am solved and bound in, through aught here on earth,
> There canst thou find me, O thou anxious thou,
> Who call'st about my gates for some lost me;
> I say my soul flowed back, became translucent.
> Search not my lips, O Love, let go my hands,
> This thing that moves as man is no more mortal.

> If thou hast seen my shade sans character,
> If thou hast seen that mirror of all moments,
> That glass to all things that o'ershadow it,
> Call not that mirror me, for I have slipped
> Your grasp, I have eluded. (Pound, 1952, p. 65)

The Keatsian entry of the soul into its objects of contemplation is cancelled by the flowing back into an illusory presence. Even the 'shade' which lies behind the 'man' is an absent reflector of 'all things'. The final 'I have eluded' leaves us not with a hidden god but with an absent centre. The poem does not theorise the division of the subject, it enacts it. Pound is content to get rid of the troublesome interference set up by the romantic selfhood which insists on being the mediator of all forms of consciousness. The mediating personae of Pound's poems are 'mere surfaces' and without character. The centre is not the speaker's character but the polysemous utterance, the openness of the text as language. Pound's concept of *logopoeia* anticipates Empson's 'ambiguity' and the post-structuralist notion of polysemy. *Logopoeia* is defined as 'the dance of the intellect among words':

> that is to say, it employs words not only for their direct meaning, but it takes count [*sic*] in a special way of habits of usage, of the context we *expect* to find with the words, its usual concomitants, of its known acceptances, and of ironical play.... It is the latest come and perhaps most tricky and undependable mode. (Pound, 1954, p. 25)

Pound's definition is highly rationalistic: the process of verbal play is fully conscious. The poet moves godlike, conducting the dance at a distance. Thus in his *theorising* Pound still acknowledges the presence of the divided speaker. The presence is the organising intelligence, the poetic craft, the hidden god. 'The supreme test of a book', wrote Pound, 'is that we should feel some unusual intelligence working behind the words.' (1954, p. 420) However, even under the hand of the Master the logopoeic mode is 'tricky and undependable'. In *practice*, released from the interference of the poet/persona, the signifying process moves towards a radical openness and an undependability which evades the consciousness of the subject, calling into question the source and nature of signification itself. Pound's masks are surfaces through which both ancient and modern voices speak in a rich polyphony. Both Pound and Eliot believed that behind the 'mere surfaces' the reader can discern the 'intelligence' or 'personality' of the poet manifested in the ordering and collocation of elements. But their radically decentred and hollowed-out poems speak to us not only of the retreat of the subject into impersonality but also of the division of the subject.

These implications are not only to be found in Anglo-American modernist writing but also in Russian Formalism during the 1920s. The early period is dominated by the work of Shklovsky whose view of poetry and whose concept of defamiliarisation have close affinities with Eliot's criticism and especially T. E. Hulme's. However, the conception of the poet as remote manipulator and self-conscious craftsman gives place to a new conception of the author as displaced subject in the writing of Mikhail Bakhtin, especially in his *Problems of Dostoevsky's Poetics* (1929, 1973). Bakhtin insists that the 'dialogic' (or polyphonic) character of Dostoevsky's novels requires the development of a new poetics. He shows that several earlier critics had recognised the presence of contradictory voices in the novels but had seen the phenomenon in terms of a multi-levelled or multi-faceted world-view. Dostoevsky's originality, argues Bakhtin, lies in his refusal to synthesise or orchestrate the polyphonic on the principle of unity. His novels do not reflect an authorial *Welt-anschauung*: 'Dostoevsky's world is profoundly *pluralistic*.' It is not merely a question of the unification of heterogenous materials but the coexistence of 'unmerged consciousnesses'. Unlike the heroes of Shakespearean drama, 'Dostoevsky's principal heroes are indeed *not only objects of the author's word, but subjects of their own directly significant word as well*' (Bakhtin, 1973, p. 4). In Tolstoy's novels, even where multiple planes exist, all the voices 'together with their fields of vision, their truths, their quests and their controversies, are immutably inscribed into the finalizing *monolithic monological whole* of the novel' (p. 59).

It would be wrong to exaggerate Bakhtin's anticipation of the post-structuralist views of Derrida, Lacan, Althusser and Kristeva. Kristeva herself, I believe, exaggerates Bakhtin's significance. Not only, as she herself points out, had he not assimilated the Freudian revolution so fundamental to the theory of the subject, but he remains firmly anchored within the Formalist problematic. The author remains an intentional subject who constructs the play of voices albeit in a new way. The dialogic principle remains an *innovation* rather than a universal principle of poetics. Bakhtin comes nearest to seeing the dialogic as a general principle in his discussion of the carnivalisation of literature. The 'carnival attitude' is expressed in a long tradition of classical literature including the Socratic dialogue and culminates in the Menippean satires of the Roman empire. Several genres are grouped in the general category of the 'Seriocomic' (Σπουδογέλοιον) and all are characterised by the 'jolly relativity' of the carnival attitude. One-sided rhetorical seriousness, rationality and singleness of meaning are weakened; identity and selfhood are split in the process of dialogic discourse.

Bakhtin's concept of the dialogic mode is a more adequate instrument for understanding poetry than the essentially monologic concepts employed by the New Critics. As we have seen, the tentative steps of Olson, Mack and others to introduce a rhetorical gap between poet and persona evoked a strong 'common-sense' reaction from the established critics in the early 1960s. The biographical fallacy, thinly disguised, was quietly readmitted at the back-door. In a sense, the reaction was soundly based. After all there were no grounds in Aristotle's *Rhetoric* for a radical split between a man's 'real self' and his rhetorical self.

Satiric Personae

In his book on Elizabethan satire, Alvin Kernan used the term 'tension' to define, not a quality of moral distance (as in New Critical usage), but the presence of contradictions in the satirist's stance. Such contradictions, it seems, would invoke Booth's strictures against moral ambiguities. However, it is interesting to find that critics have usually found ways of restoring satirists' life-enhancing mastery of their personae. W. S. Anderson adopted Kernan's five 'tensions' in an analysis of Juvenal's satires which centres on the problem of the satirist's *saeva indignatio*. A tension between (1) an appeal to rationality and (2) an irrational distortion of reality is attributed to the early satires, especially the first. Anderson argues that Juvenal eventually came to recognise the need to censor the indignant voice of the earlier satires in favour of a more rational speaker. First, he recognised, on rhetorical grounds, that an audience would 'question the ethical propriety of *indignatio* and hence of the satirist's angry picture of the Roman world.' Secondly, argues Anderson, Juvenal came to accept Seneca's argument in *De Ira* that 'indignant rhetoric presupposes a speaker who is *simulating his passion, while holding himself entirely in check*' (W. S. Anderson, pp. 158, 171, my emphasis). Subsequently, Juvenal created a new satirist (typically the satirist of the tenth and thirteenth satires) in clear conformity to the Senecan ideal of Stoic indifference. Anderson's implication is clear enough: Juvenal's adoption of the 'saner attitude of the ironic satirist' involves casting aside the mask to allow a direct expression of the authentic self, the inner self lurking behind the false selves which the exigences of rhetorical art often require. Here we have the essentials of a romantic metaphysic which is based on an absolute difference between rhetoric and authentic expression.

Such a comfortingly wholesome reading of Juvenal is severely monologic; it ignores the patent 'plurality' of even the most overtly Senecan satires. The sublime voice of the Stoic soberly praying for a sound mind in a sound body conflicts with the bitter voice of the cynic, and the malignant voice of the chauvinist and misogynist. The overall polyvalence is motivated by a rhetorical *logopoiea*, a tricky and undependable play of words. Romantic and post-romantic readings of Juvenal have been unable to recompose a unitary text. The romantic critics (Nisard and others) regarded Juvenal as the tragic victim of the decadent culture of the post-Republican world in which rhetoric supplants expressive integrity of vision. A noble vision is vitiated by a malignant rhetorical exuberance. Duff and Highet tried to revive the image of Juvenal the Stoic and proto-Christian moralist, but in doing so were forced to admit flaws, lapses and excesses in their hero. H. A. Mason comes nearest to recognising Juvenal's carnivalistic play of language, which has no respect for philosophical, moral or even psychological consistency. According to Mason, Juvenal lacks 'classic' status, because of his moral nullity (Selden, 1978, pp. 28–41). However, another reading might see the Juvenalian texts as a classic demonstration of the ultimate dominance of the signifier over the signified.

According to Roland Barthes the 'classic' text has only a 'limited plural', a polysemy which resides in connotation and is held in check by 'the old deity' denotation (Barthes, 1975, pp. 8–9). However, as we have seen, classical literature has also a subversive 'carnivalistic' tradition which has much less respect for 'the old deity'. The gap between signifier and signified, which has so fascinated the post-structuralists, is opened up already in the texts of Juvenal.

Satire, among classical forms, enforces the strongest mimetic illusion and therefore appears to cement the bond of signifier and signified most securely in the deceptive transparency of language which denotation demands. Satire demystifies and depicts 'whatever men do' (*quidquid agunt homines*) in the 'natural' language of men (the 'prosaic muse'). And yet the persona of the Juvenalian satirist is capable of an extraordinary degree of fictive autonomy. This may be regarded not as a tension in Alvin Kernan's sense but as a symptom of language's refusal of closure and transparency. This tendency to openness is, in such satire, asserted in the unstable and undepend-able nature of the persona. The instability may take the form of con-tradictions or excessiveness (usually in rhetoric) but the essential feature is the lack of a substantial, unified *presence*, of a transcen-dental subject immanent in the text.

It is true that the writing of Juvenal's important predecessor, Horace, is more evidently 'classic' in its respect for the old deity denotation. The sense (the illusion) of a full presence is strongly enforced by the text's adherence to a plain-style norm of language, by the regular insertion of candid autobiographical references, and by the author's declared faith in the transparency of language ('Attend to the subject matter and the words will look after them-selves'). (Selden, 1978) However, the limitation of the classic text's plurality does not make the concept of its authenticity any less pro-blematic.

The satires of the Elizabethan, John Marston, raise in a more extreme form the questions we have considered in relation to Juvenal. Marston's satirist is a bitter malcontent, who adds a Calvinistic pessimism to the Roman's malice. The satirist's persona declares itself boldly as a fictional product, an exuberant and heightened development of the Elizabethan wild-man of the woods, the savage castigator of mortal vice. However, the voice is desta-bilised in several ways. The anger is oddly undermined by Marston's

open pessimism. The incorrigible sinfulness of man seems to leave
no adequate motive for the satirist's self-righteous denunciations. In
Certaine Satyres (1598) Marston concludes by abandoning satire for
the Stoic's serenity and detachment:

> I'le slumber out my time in discontent,
> And never wake to be malevolent,
> A beedle to the worlds impuritie;
> But ever sleepe in still securitie. (p. 92)

But, in the *Scourge of Villanie* (1598), the opposite stance is openly
embraced:

> Preach not the Stoickes patience to me,
> I hate no man, but mens impietie.
> My soule is vext, what power will'th desist?
> Or dares to stop a sharpe fangd satirist? (p. 106)

Anthony Caputi resolves this apparent contradiction by disentang-
ling Marston's 'real' voice of Stoic teacher-philosopher from the
'artificial' mask of the indignant satyr-satirist. Only by resolving the
fictional persona into 'rhetorical' and 'authentic' components can
Marston's satirist be restored to the required rational (monologic)
coherence. This solution is no more satisfactory than W. S. Anderson's rehabilitation of Juvenal.

The example of satire has been considered in some detail, not
because it is in any way exceptional, but because it presents in sharp
relief the *general* problem of theorising the author/text relationship.
The formal impersonality of much prose fiction and drama has dis-
couraged the application of expressive and crudely psychological
interpretations in those genres. But, as we have seen, even when the
New Critics founded their discipline upon Eliot's theory of impersonality, they soon found themselves settling slowly upon the bedrock of a metaphysic which had never been seriously challenged. It
may turn out that literary criticism cannot survive such a challenge,
or that the theory of the subject proposed by Lacan and Kristeva is a
form of knowledge which cannot be directly appropriated by literary
critics. The practices and procedures of close reading of texts present
quite different possibilities and criteria for validation and agreement

among practitioners from those available to psychoanalysts. Nevertheless, the radical perspective of the post-structuralists cannot simply be ignored. We may have to reconsider as critics, some of the assumptions underlying our practices.

Existentialism: the Survival of the 'Subject'

Before considering the important contribution of the structuralists to the theory of the subject and the effects of their contribution on concepts of persona and authorship, it will be helpful to establish the outline of an existentialist view, against which the work of Lacan, Derrida and Kristeva can be seen as a reaction. An existentialist position retains the classic presupposition of a 'transcendental subject' (that is, a subject which is a substantial and fixed constituent in the subject–object relation) but denies the subject a pre-existent identity. Sartre's pronouncement about the priority of existence over essence suggests a model according to which a man's role-playing is part of a life-long search for, or rather *choice* of, an authentic self.

Sartre's view of the voyage of self-definition may be regarded as a secularised development of the religious existentialism of Søren Kierkegaard, who believed that the category of the 'individual' was the key to the conversion of men to the Christian religion: 'For one can guarantee to make a Christian of every man he can get to come under this category.' (Kierkegaard, p. 135) Until a man's psychosomatic entity has been transformed by the mediation of the 'self' which is in turn posited by the 'spirit', then he remains a mere 'it' and not a 'free' individual. For Sartre, man has no spiritual essence; his own essence is his freedom. He is pure negativity: his nature is not fixed and universal but is only what he makes it. Our nothingness is also our freedom. To behave as if we are *something*, to deny by our actions our freedom to choose, is an act of 'bad faith'. The man who believes he *is* a waiter, to take Sartre's example, denies both his freedom and his nothingness.

Sartre believes that we have no metaphysical substratum of individual identity or soul, but, from the moment of our entry into existence, we are compelled to choose an existence: our lives and our actions are determined by our interpretation of the world. In this sense we are 'condemned to be free'. Each individual is a centre of consciousness, but is, at the same time, without a centre; on the one hand the world is structured by my way of seeing, but on the other hand, consciousness itself is only capable of a negative definition – it has no identity of its own (no *en-soi*) but is always *of* something external to itself which it is not. Our consciousness is identical with these nihilations of the objects of consciousness: 'we are what we are not'. Despite this negative definition of consciousness, Sartre preserves the metaphysical primacy of individual consciousness in his notion of the 'original project', which is required in order to answer the question 'Why do I choose to do this and not that? What connects the choices that make up my life?' Finding the Freudian and Marxian solutions to these questions over-general in their determinism, Sartre is compelled to introduce this evidently metaphysical concept. The project is the principle of unity through which an individual life is constituted as a totality rather than as a seriality. Each of my choices is related to a larger choice, a 'free and global project' of which the individual choices are repetitions and increments. It is not surprising that Sartre has spent so much of his time in writing critical biographies, notably of Baudelaire, Genet and Flaubert. A literary work is analysed as an *act* which is then related to the writer's original project. The two aspects are synthesised both subjectively (biographically) and objectively (in terms of social determinants) (see Hahn).

The genesis of the original project must remain a mystery. Here we enter an obscure terrain adjacent to the worlds of vitalism and mysticism. We are left with a potent and influential humanism which places the highest value on the individual's existential *authenticity*. A substantial school of criticism (the Geneva school) shares Sartre's phenomenological perspective and in effect regards a writer's work as the ongoing expression of an original project. This amounts to a new form of the biographical approach to criticism. The genesis of the text is not sought externally in a biographical history but in the structures of consciousness which are immanent in the text. In Hillis Miller's reading of Hardy, the novelist's works form a total project structured according to contradictory modes of consciousness ('distance' and 'desire'). The relation between the author and the personages in the writings is not seen as problematic. Sartre's arguments against authorial intrusion in the presentation of subjective points of view leaves unspecified the origin of the 'subjectivités-points-de-vue'. In effect we are left with the requirement of an illusion of an authentic *prise de conscience* (sense of contingency).

Sartre, and psychoanalytic thinkers in his tradition, such as Laing and Szasz, presuppose the very thing which is in question   the transcendental subject. Such a subject is for them a *sine qua non* of the phenomenological enterprise, the unmoved mover within each perceptual universe. Sartre's concept of 'freedom' cancels the decentred 'nothingness' and recentres it in an original project. In Lacan the concept of negativity (absence, lack) displaces the very concept of 'centre'. While Sartre had attempted ambitious totalisations in his critical biographies, the post-structuralist critics characterise literary works as open structures whose centres are radically displaced; their crucial determinations are not biographical but linguistic (in a new enlarged sense).

Lacan: the Displacement of the 'Subject'

In *Krapp's Last Tape* the elderly Krapp listens to his recorded voice of thirty years before. His basic drives and addictions remain with him (bananas, alcohol and sex), but the self he was fails to connect with what he has become: 'Just been listening to that stupid bastard I took myself for thirty years ago, hard to believe I was ever as bad as that. Thank God that's all done with anyway.' (Beckett, p. 17) He is wrong about his appetites ('How do you manage it, she said, at your age?') but right about his 'personality'. Not only does his old confident and romantic self strike him as unbelievably alien but even his earlier vocabulary is foreign to him. He has to look up 'viduity' in the dictionary and savours the word 'spool' as if for the first time. The discontinuity between old and new self, like the abrupt discontinuities in the characters between the two parts of *Waiting for Godot* places a question mark over the ontological standing of the 'self' in its every guise and form. It is not surprising to find that many critics have been able to recognise this negativity in Beckett only as a kind of zero point, the theoretical nadir of human consciousness, from which one may then permit oneself a new beginning. Peter Brook sees Beckett's darkness as the wish for light: 'Beckett does not say "no" with satisfaction; he forges his merciless

"no" out of a longing for "yes" and so his despair is the negative
from which the contour of its opposite can be drawn.' (Brook, p. 65)
But it is surely more legitimate to see Beckett as a post-humanist
rather than as a neo-humanist. The more significant moment in
Endgame from the point of view of consciousness is Hamm's sudden
recognition towards the end of the play of his existential decentredness:

> HAMM: I was never there.
> CLOV: Lucky for you.
>   *He looks out of window.*
> HAMM: Absent, always. It all happened without me.
>   I don't know what's happened.

Commenting on *Endgame*, Theodor Adorno declares:

> The catastrophes which are the inspiration of *Endgame* have
> exploded the individual, whose substantiality and absoluteness
> provided the common ground for Kierkegaard, Jaspers and the
> Sartrean version of Existentialism. . . . The individual, both
> the result of the capitalist process of alienation and the stub-
> born protest against it, reveals its ephemeral character as an
> historical category. (Adorno, pp. 89–90)

The emptying of the category of the individual is here seen as having
specific historical determinations: its death is brought on by 'cata-
strophes' and by the experience of extreme alienation under twentieth-century capitalism. A post-structuralist would argue that
'individuality' is only an historical form of the more general category
of the 'subject', that site where the 'soul', 'individuality' and the
'inner self' have flowered.

The traditional humanist view of language is comfortingly anthropocentric: nothing is more expressive of man's centrality in the
world than language. The Word was made flesh. The style is the
man. The pen is mightier than the sword. Above all things our
century is the time of the word, the symbol, the sign. And yet the
Empire of Linguistics has emptied the world of its privileged
categories, including the 'human'. The connection between 'anti-
humanism' and the dominion of language can be seen in the writings
of Robbe-Grillet, in which a phase of polemical *chosisme* (the an-

nouncement of a world of non-tragic, non-anthropocentric 'things')
is succeeded by a phase in which novels are seen not as representa-
tions but as self-referential demonstrations of the process of textual
signification. Man ceases to be the centre and language ceases to be a
transparent reflector (Heath, pp. 67–9).

Nietzsche founded his philosophy on a concept of nihilism – on
the sense that 'Everything lacks meaning'. Despite the mysterious
animism of that 'will to power' with which he fills the void left by
meaning, Nietzsche's critique of the entire history of Western
metaphysics anticipates remarkably those of Derrida, Foucault and
Lacan. First, Nietzsche rejects the subject as cause and point of
origin (Nietzsche, pp. 268–70). Secondly, the causal relationship
between things and words is severed. Language is essentially poetic,
giving us a poetic transposition of the 'real' (see Stern, p. 136).
Nietzsche's deconstruction of 'truth', of the epistemology of subject
and object, and of causality, is an essentially *negative* move; there is
no theorising of the construction of 'meanings' in particular historical societies. The fictionality of 'truth' leads Nietzsche to celebrate
the artist as the highest being in whom the 'will to power' finds its
most energetic channel of expression. Nietzsche's final move is
always to abandon the rational promptings of his critique of Western
philosophy in favour of a dogmatic assertion of the subversive 'will
to power'. The *theorising* of the decentred subject awaited the
Freudian revolution.

There is little doubt that Jacques Lacan's sibylline leaves are the
key to an understanding of the most radical developments in the
theory of the subject. The selection of *Écrits* in 1977 made the
essential texts available for the first time in English. Lacan provides
a reading of Freud which focuses attention on Freud's scientific
achievement, the discovery of the unconscious. This discovery, this
'Copernican' revolution in our understanding of the subject, has
been obscured, according to Lacan, by an exclusive emphasis on
biological determinism in the work of Anglo-American psychoanalysts and by neglect of the radical implications of the theory.
According to Lacan, we pass from the earliest auto-erotic state of
infanthood, in which interior and exterior aspects of sense data are
undifferentiated, to the 'Mirror Phase', when the 'I' is precipitated
into being by an identification with its own body-image. Then, the
pre-Oedipal phase of identification with the mother is followed by

the first signs of an existential anxiety intensified by the periodic absence of the mother. The beginnings of language are manifested at this stage, for example in the celebrated *fort/da* game (cited by Freud) in which the child symbolises its wished-for control over the mother's presence by uttering the word *da* (here) as it draws a cotton-reel to itself and the word *fort* (gone) as it throws it away again.

This first appearance of language is also the moment of the child's entry into the 'symbolic order', the *system* of language. Lacan adopts the normal structuralist view that the signifier has no incarnational unity with the signified. The *fort/da* game is *already*, in its marking of presence and absence, a speech from the unconscious, or as Lacan puts it, 'This is the point of insertion of a symbolic order that *pre-exists the infantile subject and in accordance with which he will have to structure himself.*' (Lacan, p. 234) It is central to Lacan's reading of Freud that the unconscious is structured like a language. A dream, according to Freud, is a 'rebus' (an enigmatical representation of a word in pictorial images). Lacan develops Freud's structural concepts in *The Interpretation of Dreams* by aligning them with linguistic concepts (signifier/signified, metaphor/metonymy). It is the primacy in the unconscious of this signifying mechanism which entails the dissolving of the transcendental subject. The 'sliding of the signified under the signifier' undermines the unified subject, that *cogito* which has dominated Western philosophy since the seventeenth century. In language and in literature, the 'word' is never a full presence, never dissolves the 'bar' between signifier and signified.

In his references to metaphor and metonymy, Lacan acknowledges his debt to Jakobson's celebrated essay on the relations between the two figures of speech and two kinds of aphasia. Jakobson in turn drew upon Saussure's basic distinction between the two axes of language, the vertical and horizontal planes (echoing the synchronic and diachronic), which allow substitution (as in metaphor) of one signifier for another, and combination (as in metonymy) of one signifier with another. Jakobson also suggested that the principle of metaphoric substitution underlay the 'poetic' function and that the principle of metonymic association underlay the 'realistic' mode of representation. Lacan's relocation of the linguistic mechanism in the Freudian unconscious (the dream is only one convenient text for the analyst) has profound implications for the 'author' of the text, the subject: 'Is the place that I occupy as the subject of a signifier concentric or excentric, in relation to the place I occupy as subject of the signified? – that is the question.' (Lacan, p. 165) Lacan uncovers the conceptual homology between Jakobson's division of linguistic processes between metaphor and metonymy and Freud's division of the dream-work between 'condensation' and 'displacement'. The significance is far-reaching: not only is the pre-existing language system, into which we are precipitated in infancy, structured in accordance with the unstable order of the sign, but the subject itself emerges from the same process. The subject is absent until it produces itself, decentred in the structure which already includes it. The subject's own identity is achieved by that gradual process of identification and differentiation which the infant undergoes. The *fort/da* game is an example of the early merging of linguistic and subjective modes. The phonemic difference between 'o' and 'a' refers to the absence and presence of the mother. But the order of the signifier ('o' and 'a') does not coincide with the order of the signified (absence and presence).

How is it, then, that the sliding of the signified under the signifier does not prevent the very process of signification from taking place? How is it that 'I' can intend a meaning, linking signifier and signified in a (momentary) fix? It is not possible here to elaborate Lacan's reading of Freud's theories of the subject's emergence in the process of identification, repression and desire (see Coward and Ellis; Lemaire; Burniston). The most important stage in the formation of the subject, according to Lacan, is the finally constitutive entry into the symbolic which occurs when the infant submits to the paternal authority and accepts a *position* in the family as 'son' or 'daughter'. This positionality (sexual and familial) is the basis for the possibility of signification. The establishing of the *place* of the subject is at the same time the full entry into the symbolic order (language), where 'I' may now speak itself and thereby permit the coincidence of signifier and signified in intended 'meaning'. However, 'I' am never where I think; my positionality in the symbolic order is at the axis of the signifier and the signified. Such a position makes the jointing of the levels possible, but the signification is always interrupted and undermined:

This signifying game between metonymy and metaphor, up to and including the active edge that splits my desire between a

refusal of the signifier and a lack of being, and links my fate to
the question of my destiny, this game, in all its inexorable
subtlety, is played until the match is called, there where I am
not, because I cannot situate myself there. (Lacan, p. 166)

All discourse is a *demand* in the face of a 'lack of being' (that sense
of lack which is the inevitable concomitant of the infant's first
recognition of identity). The demand, addressed to the Other (originally the mother), is the articulation (in the symbolic order) of a need
or appetite. The articulation of demand in signifiers opens up the
metonymic process which in turn produces a sense of loss and of the
Other's inadequacy. Lacan calls this metonymic process 'desire',
which is not centred in the subject but is the 'excentric' and
insatiable unconscious itself.

Lacan's own text is a realisation of his theory of the subject. He
refuses to acknowledge a 'signified' – a theory which his text is
'about'. Instead, he allows the free play of signification to split and
decentre his own text. Puns, word-play, condensation and displacement leave the text as ambiguous and treacherous as that unconscious to which he alludes. The splitting of the subject is ingeniously
evoked by the speech of 'the Freudian thing' (the unconscious) and
of the desk (another 'it'). Lacan is drawing attention, somewhat perversely, to the fact that speech is always a 'discourse of the Other',
that the subject is not the origin of discourse but only its place.

The effect of Lacan's ideas has been to call the old philosophy in
doubt. We are left with an unanswered question rather than with a
new perspective. At any rate this is the prospect offered by Jacques
Derrida. His message is clear: the metaphysics of presence has
dominated Western thought since Plato. After Nietzsche and Freud,
the notion that the ego is a substantial unity and the origin of all
discourse can no longer be the unquestioned (and even unthought)
metaphysical basis of all philosophy:

> It would be possible to show that all the names related to
> fundamentals, to principles, or to the centre have always de-
> signated the constant of a presence – *eidos archè, telos, energeia,
> ousia* (essence, existence, substance, subject), *aletheia*, trans-
> cendentality, consciousness, or conscience, Gòd, man, and so
> forth. (Derrida, 1970, p. 249)

Derrida recognises the difficulty (impossibility) of destroying the metaphysical matrix of Western thought without employing meta-physical concepts in the process. A similar problem arises if we attempt to supersede the doctrine of the substantial unity of the subject (soul/inner self/ego).

Because the literary text offers itself as an individual project, it has had the historical function of preserving the very concept of a trans-cendental subject. Like that ultimate Subject, God, the presence of the ordinary subject is incarnated in the word, the *logos*. Rhetorical theories recognise the artifice involved in the projections of the self, but still retain the metaphysics of presence. The Romantics erased even that gap of projection in their philosophy of spiritual expression and total presence.

Lacan's impenetrable, ambiguous and treacherous text is a re-markable attempt to construct a decentred discourse. It is significant that the major texts of modernism (Yeats, Pound, Joyce, Eliot, Beckett) also speak of an absent subject, albeit not in concepts but in the very verbal play of the discourse. The history of metaphysics is not absent from their discourses but is cast like driftwood upon the sand of a strange new-found land.

In Derrida's view, 'writing' itself is the general condition of all signifying practices. Western philosophy has consistently *repressed* writing in favour of speech (*logos*). 'Speech' in its immediacy pro-mises a full presence, an instant gratification, while 'writing' is a substitution, a deferment. But, in the face of the lack of presence, the writer (Rousseau is Derrida's text) 'describes the passage to writing as the restoration, by a certain absence and by a sort of calculated effacement, of presence disappointed of itself in speech.' (Derrida, 1976, p. 142) The 'restoration . . . of presence' is, of course, an illusion: 'writing' merely supplements and replaces an already absent presence: 'Writing consecrates the dispossession that had already dislocated the spoken word.' (p. 166)

It is one of the surprising conjunctures of intellectual history that Marxist philosophy has undergone its most significant revolution as a result of an encounter with Lacan's Freud and with linguistics. Althusser introduces a new Marxist theory of the subject (via Lacan) according to which individuals are inserted as 'subjects' within the ideological apparatuses which constitute the State (even a communist state). In 'Ideology and the State' (1970) Althusser in effect compares 'ideology' (that 'common sense' which gives us the 'real') with the Freudian unconscious in its function of constituting the 'subject'. As social individuals we 'recognise' ourself as 'subjects' through the categories of ideology: 'All ideology hails or interpellates concrete individuals as concrete subjects.' (Althusser, 1971, p. 162) It should be stressed that here Althusser is talking of the *general functioning of ideology at all times*. He recognises that the apparatuses through which the individual is interpellated as a subject will have different forms in different cultures, but he is concerned to define the structure of ideology in general, on the analogy with the structure of the unconscious. The most radical emphasis is upon the preformed programme which awaits the subject:

> Before its birth, the child is therefore always-already a subject, appointed as a subject in and by the specific familial ideological configuration in which it is 'expected' once it has been conceived. I hardly need add that this familial ideological configuration is, in its uniqueness, highly structured, and that it is in this implacable ... structure that the former subject-to-be will have to 'find' 'its' place, i.e. 'become' the sexual subject (boy or girl) which it already is in advance. (p. 165)

The 'Subject' and the Plural Text

At this juncture, it is in order to reflect on the implications of Lacan's and Althusser's conceptual placing of the subject from the point of view of literary criticism. Formulations, such as 'the author creates an art object', 'the author expresses his meaning', and 'the text's determinate meaning is', are superseded by new formulations which acknowledge a structure of determinations (including literary, linguistic and cultural) which permit neither premature closures of the text's significations nor the centering of determinate meanings on an authorial identity. The text's plurality entails the devalorisation of the author.

Where does this leave critical evaluation, the concepts of innovation and determinate meaning? The negative challenge of Barthes and Lacan is a powerful one, but positive conclusions are less easily drawn. Barthes's aesthetic is oriented towards indeterminacy, that 'pleasure' of the text which exceeds any social or structural function.

This 'ideal text' is triumphantly plural and refuses all closure. A text is an interweaving of 'codes' which are the traces of the *'already written'*, traces which converge and intersect in 'writing'; a text is an opening into a process. Literature itself is 'never anything but a single text' and a particular text is not a discrete example of literature but an 'entrance into a network with a thousand entrances'. For Barthes, reading a text is not a process of *knowing* but a setting the text in motion in order to realise meanings, none of which are definitive:

> To read is to find meanings, and to find meanings is to name them; but these named meanings are swept towards other names; names call to each other, reassemble, and their group- ing calls for further naming: I name, I unname, I rename: so the text passes: it is a nomination in the course of becoming, a tireless approximation, a metonymic labor. (1975, p. 11)

Barthes's critique of the classic realist text convinces us (1) that the realistic text naturalises language through the innocent devices of narrative and logic; (2) that even in the classic text, where the voices are assigned an origin, there exists the trace of a limited plurality in that play of connotation which steadily undermines the illusion of denotation; and (3) that the reading even of a realist text cannot arrive at a totality of meaning(s) or the 'truth'. Barthes comes nearest to a totalising view when he announces his intention of proposing 'the semantic substance . . . of several kinds of criticism (psychologi- cal, psychoanalytical, thematic, historical, structural)'. Each kind of criticism may, *if it wishes*, come into play in listening in to one of the text's voices, but totalisation itself is resisted as an ideological trap which might concede the text its claimed 'naturalness'. Barthes's concept of 'closure' undermines the view of criticism as knowledge. The 'illusion' of denotation which pervades the classic text is the effect of the arbitrary closure of the signifying process. Signifier and signified come together in momentary identity only as a result of a *limitation* of the inherent productivity of language.

In contrast to Barthes, Althusser envisages the possibility of a discourse which can be detached from ideology, namely the subject- less discourse of a 'science'. Althusser considers that we require a *knowledge* of art, its processes, and especially its relation to ideology.

He regards major literature as having not a scientific but a critical relationship to ideology. The novels of Balzac and Solzhenitsyn achieve 'a view which presupposes a *retreat*, an *internal distantiation* from the very ideology from which their novels emerged'. (Althusser, 1971, p. 204) The source of this remarkable effect is not entirely clear, but there is no suggestion that the novelists were able to stand outside their places as subjects of ideology: only because Balzac 'stuck to his political ideology could he produce *in it* this internal "distance", which gives us a critical "view" of it.' (p. 206) Althusser suggests that a 'scientific' knowledge of art would uncover the 'processes which produce the "aesthetic" effect of a work of art'.

Pierre Macherey, Althusser's disciple, has attempted to arrive at such a knowledge in his *Pour une théorie de la production littéraire* (1966). Macherey offers a Lacanian reading of the literary text as a 'decentred' discourse. The 'incompleteness' of a text is determined by its ideological horizon. The writer, far from being a romantic free spirit expressing his or her inner self, is an ideological subject, whose discourse is necessarily hollowed and pitted with absences, silences and hiatuses. The silences (the things which cannot be said) speak of that ideological structure which produced the text. On this view, the *origin* of the text does not lie in the subject (the author) but in the ideological process. He argues that literary texts can no longer be regarded as closed and completed structures of meaning and must now be treated as symptomatic discourses like those of the psycho-analytic patient whose discourse is read for what is *not* said and for what is suppressed through the metonymic and metaphoric processes of displacement and condensation. Only by thus shifting our ground can we establish a *knowledge* of the way in which literature and ideology are related. This argument has been powerfully supported and developed by Terry Eagleton in *Criticism and Ideology*. As we have seen, he argues that Macherey (and Althusser) over-privilege 'art' by granting it a unique status midway between ideology and science. Eagleton firmly reinserts the literary text in the domain of ideology, granting it a distinctive power of reworking the materials of ideology and even of producing an 'ideology of the text', but refusing it the *kind* of relative autonomy suggested by Althusser. Eagleton accepts the analogy between a scientific reading of the text and the Freudian reading of the dream's deep layer; both readings involve theorising the text's (dream's) mode of production (the dream-work).

The authorial ideology is, in Eagleton's view, one determinate discourse among a number of articulated ideological discourses which form a possibly heterogeneous or contradictory 'conjuncture'. While accepting the concept of a decentred subject, he conceives the *place* of the subject in a more determinate manner than Barthes or Derrida. The plurality of the text is a determinate plurality, an over-determined conjuncture rather than a 'free' play of significations. In this, his position resembles Althusser's, but must, in my view, be sharply distinguished from Lacan's, who only provides conceptual material for Althusser's theory of the subject's insertion in ideology. The apparent closeness of Marxist and Lacanian theories conceals a radical difference in their problematics. In the former, the subject is inserted into a complexly structured social formation; the decentering of the subject is understood in the context of a global historical *problématic*. Men are the 'bearers' (Marx's *träger*) of a structural position in specific intersections of determinants. In Lacan the subject is much less determinate *as a position*; the unconscious has a poetic trickiness in its disordering of the subject. A simple equating of ideology/social formation and the unconscious is quite illegitimate. The specificity of social formations involves a different mode of materiality from the specificity of the discourses of the unconscious. Any premature collapsing or even combining of materialist and psychoanalytic concepts will not solve the problem. Marxism may need a theory of the subject, but it cannot be simply imported.

It must be admitted that no one has succeeded in drawing from Lacan's theories definite conclusions about the role of the subject in the *production* of literary texts. Julia Kristeva has gone beyond the Althusserian perspective in a suggestive way by showing that in poetical language the interpellation of the subject is threatened by a pre-symbolic set of drives which is subversive of the stable positioning of the subject in the symbolic order. The transgression of grammatical rules in poetical language signifies the perpetual unmaking of the subject and is a manifestation of that insatiable semiotic play which is the precondition of the symbolic order. In poetic language especially, the speaking subject shows its capacity for transgression and renewal of the order in which it is caught. While literary criticism may be able to recognise this 'renewal' in stylistic and cultural terms, it is unlikely to be able to do so in the psychoanalytic terms required by Kristeva.

In her view, any systematic order is necessarily exposed to and undermined by 'heterogeneous' processes in the form both of biophysical drives and of the material 'outside' (Coward and Ellis, ch. 7). The apparent naturalness and stability of such orders is guaranteed by an ideology of transcendental subjectivity. According to Kristeva, a genuinely materialist account of culture and society must abandon the premise of a unified subject. In her view, *this is not less true of the semanalyst*:

> The subject of the semiotic metalanguage must, however briefly, call himself in question, must emerge from the protective shell of a transcendental ego within a logical system, and so restore his connexion with that negativity – drive-governed, but also social, political and historical – which rends and renews the social code. (Kristeva, 1973, p. 1250)

'Knowledge' here becomes a profoundly problematic concept. In Barthes's view (of 1963) the metalanguage of criticism does not 'discover' the text but 'covers' it. The critic adjusts the metalanguages of his time (existentialism, psychoanalysis or Marxism) to the language of the text (constrained as it is by the logico-systematic forms of its time). (Barthes, 1972, p. 259) Criticism is seen as a kind of hedonistic 'play' by Barthes and as a risky intervention by Kristeva. Neither writer allows the critic to *fix* the text as a conjuncture of formal and historical determinations. Kristeva's concept of poetry's transgression and renewal does not include the renewal of the literary system itself, but only the transgression of the social law. The privileging of the psychoanalytic metalanguage and the normalising of 'plurality' and *'jouissance'* impose substantial constraints upon *historical* criticism with respect to both its objects and its conceptual capability.

When compared with the literary history of Auerbach or Curtius, the backward glances afforded by Barthes and Kristeva are curiously foreshortened. The broad oppositions, denotation/connotation, closure/plurality, even when qualified, leave one with an unsatisfactory and oddly rhetorical reading of literary history. The *avant-garde* text becomes normative and the classic text redeemable only in spite of itself. The concept of the classic text's 'limited plural' is carefully distinguished from the plural of the modern text, and yet the categories are difficult to preserve. The instability of voices in the satires of Juvenal and Marston, and the linguistic hedonism of Rabelais, the metaphysical poets and Sterne already point to the incursions of the heterogeneous. One might find the opposition between the 'readerly' and the 'writerly' text useful as a synchronic model of early-seventeenth-century poetry: Ben Jonson's 'readerly' poetry insists on the primacy of denotation, while Andrew Marvell's 'writerly' texts defer denotation and promote that 'pleasure' of the text to which Barthes refers. The difficulty for literary criticism is not in accepting the concept of transgressive texts but in acceding to the (Lacanian) theoretical underpinning of the concept. The Lacanian perspective may give the critic a way of reading those texts which before had been dismissed as inauthentic, disintegrated or disorganised. Certain structural shifts, gaps and indeterminacies may now be seen as necessary effects of ideological and biophysical processes. However, the theorising of the action of presymbolic drives seems necessarily to belong outside the scope of literary criticism. Shoshana Felman has argued that psychoanalytic criticism, in its Lacanian form, is *textual* and not extrinsic or reductive (Felman, p. 142). However, even if one were satisfied that Lacanian theory could legitimately extend its domain beyond its clinical locus, its textualising of history remains a major impediment. In my view, the distinctive multivalence of Andrew Marvell's poems is related to the historical conditions of their production (Selden, 1972). From a post-structuralist point of view, the concept of historical conditions has no *authority*, but merely refers to a discursive strategy, which imposes relatively arbitrary constructions upon the infinite text of history as if they were objective elements.

Althusser's concept of a decentred 'structure in dominance' offers a way forward for the literary critic who has abandoned the notion of organic texts and univocal meaning, but who cannot adopt the Lacanian perspective. The text, then, is decentred within a structure of determinations, one of which is the relatively autonomous level of 'the literary'. In previous chapters, I have discussed the text's conditions of production and reception. It may now seem necessary to introduce a semiotic level to take account of the biophysical drives or the differential nature of signs which disrupt and displace not only authorial discourse but also the reader's commentary. However, one cannot simply 'insert' a semiotic level. Once we admit the ultimate indeterminacy of meaning, we transform history into a 'general text', which can possess no determinate levels or structure.

Jonathan Culler has argued that Derrida's theory does not make the production of meaning pointless:

> What deconstruction proposes is not an end to distinctions, not an indeterminacy that makes meaning the invention of the reader. The play of meaning is the result of . . . the 'play of the world', in which the general text always provides further connections, correlations, and contexts. (Culler, 1983, p. 134)

From this point of view, no ways of inscribing the 'text' of history possess authority; particular inscriptions merely set the play of meaning going in one particular direction rather than another. Barbara Johnson has posed the problem very clearly:

> In saying that history is fiction, a text subject to ideological skewings and mystifications, and that it cannot be relied upon as a source of objective knowledge, deconstructive theory sometimes seems to block all access to the possibility of reading explicitly 'referential' documents in conjunction with literary or speculative texts.... The question ... is how to use history and biography deconstructively, how to seek in them not answers, ... but new questions and new ways in which the literary and non-literary texts alike can be made to read and to rework each other. (B. Johnson, p. 13)

It is noticeable that the mere engagement with this problem compels Professor Johnson to conduct her discourse through the binary logic which the deconstructive practice seeks to displace. She would no doubt agree that 'source', 'objective knowledge', 'referential', 'non-literary', all require to be written 'sous rature' (under erasure), and yet one cannot help believing that this self-denying ordinance entails a perverse anti-discourse, which unties itself as it articulates itself. The problem posed by Professor Johnson presupposes the very distinction between the literary and the extraliterary which is denied in her solution which seeks to implicate the historical in the literary so as to produce an agitation in the 'general text'.

The discourse of this book has, perhaps deviously (obviously, from a deconstructor's viewpoint), asserted the 'objectivity' of historical criticism by suggesting that the indeterminacies of writing and reading are grounded in the structural plurality of conjunctures. The concept of conjuncture requires us to preserve levels of discourse each responsive to the specific effectivity of particular practices. The critic cannot finally interpret texts, because they are necessarily decentred. The instability of a text's voices can be understood as the textual effect of overdetermination, defined in historical rather than psychoanalytic terms. The plurality of the text is an aspect of its position within a field of determinations. This perspective will yield no final textual meaning. The critic need no longer be exercised by the problem of origins. Texts will no longer trouble us with their untidy excess, their tendency to speak as if from another place than their apparent origin in the author's 'inner self'. The semiotic revolution has at least established conclusively that literary texts are not closed systems but relatively open structures. By removing texts from their historical locations (or by deconstructing history), the post-structuralists have forced themselves to overlook the possibility that the plurality of texts is necessitated by their historical conditions of production, and that the plurality of readings is also an aspect of the historical placing of the subject in and between ideological positions. The decentering of the text and the displacement of the subject as origin and source of meaning does not leave us with a chaotic field of arbitrarily conflicting or interweaving codes but with a more complexly structured discourse and a less unified concept of meaning.

Note

1 Vol. 3, no. 2 (1966), pp. 89–153. A similar collection of papers on 'Personae in Donne' was published in *Southern Quarterly*, 14 (1976), 173–213.

Bibliography

Abrams, M. H., *Natural Supernaturalism* (New York, 1971).

Adlam, Diana, *et al.* (editorial board), 'Psychology, ideology and the human subject', *Ideology and Consciousness*, 1 (May 1977), 5–56.

Adorno, Theodor W., 'Towards an understanding of *Endgame*', in B. G. Chevigny (ed.), *Twentieth Century Interpretations of Endgame* (Englewood Cliffs, NJ, 1969), pp. 82–114.

Althusser, Louis, *For Marx*, trans. B. Brewster (London, 1969).

Althusser, Louis, *Reading Capital*, trans. B. Brewster (London, 1970).

Althusser, Louis, *Lenin and Philosophy and Other Essays*, trans. B. Brewster (London, 1971).

Althusser, Louis, *Essays in Self-Criticism*, trans. G. Lock (London, 1976).

Anderson, Perry, *Lineages of the Absolutist State* (London, 1974a).

Anderson, Perry, *Passages from Antiquity to Feudalism* (London, 1974b).

Anderson, Perry, *Considerations on Western Marxism* (London, 1976).

Anderson, Perry, *Arguments within English Marxism* (London, 1980).

Anderson, W. S., 'Anger in Juvenal and Seneca', *Univ. of California Publications in Classical Philology*, 19, iii (1964), 127–96.

Bakhtin, Mikhail, *Problems of Dostoevsky's Poetics*, trans. R. W. Rotsel (Ann Arbor, Mich., 1973).

Bann, S. and Bowlt, J. E. (eds), *Russian Formalism* (Edinburgh, 1973).

Barthes, Roland, *Writing Degree Zero*, trans. A. Lavers and C. Smith (London, 1967).

Barthes, Roland, *Critical Essays*, trans. R. Howard (Evanston, Ill., 1972).

Barthes, Roland, *S/Z*, trans. R. Miller (London, 1975, French original 1970).

Bateson, F. W., *Wordsworth: a Re-Interpretation* (2nd edn, London, 1956).

Beckett, Samuel, *Krapp's Last Tape and Embers* (London, 1965).

Belsey, Catherine, *Critical Practice* (London and New York, 1980).

Bennett, Tony, *Formalism and Marxism* (London and New York, 1979).

Bhaskar, Roy, 'Feyerabend and Bachelard: two philosophies of science', *New Left Review*, 94 (November–December 1975), 31–55.

Bleich, David, *Subjective Criticism* (Baltimore and London, 1978).

Bloom, Harold, *The Anxiety of Influence: a Theory of Poetry* (New York and London, 1973).

Bond, Edward, *Bingo: Scenes of Money and Death* (London, 1974).

Booth, Wayne C., *The Rhetoric of Fiction* (Chicago, Ill., 1961).

Bouret, Jean, *Degas*, trans. D. Woodward (London, 1965).

Brewster, Ben, 'From *Novy Lef* with an introduction', *Screen*, 12, iv (1971/2), 59–102.

Brook, Peter, *The Empty Space* (London, 1968, 1972).

Burniston, S. and Weedon, C., 'Ideology, subjectivity and the artistic text', *Working Papers in Cultural Studies*, 10 (1977), 216–22.

Canguilhem, Georges, 'What is a scientific ideology', trans. M. Shortland, *Radical Philosophy*, 29 (autumn 1981), 20–5.

Carr, Stephen L., 'The ideology of antithesis: science versus literature and the exemplary case of J. S. Mill', *Modern Language Quarterly*, 42 (1981), 247–64.

Casey, John, *The Language of Criticism* (London, 1966).

Collingwood, R. G., *An Autobiography* (1939, Oxford, 1970).

Cousins, Mark, 'The logic of deconstruction', *Oxford Literary Review*, 3, ii (1978), 70–7.

Coward, Rosalind, and Ellis, John, *Language and Materialism. Developments in Semiology and the Theory of the Subject* (London, 1977).

Culler, Jonathan, *Structuralist Poetics* (London, 1975).

Culler, Jonathan, *The Pursuit of Signs. Semiotics, Literature, Deconstruction* (London and Henley, 1981).

Culler, Jonathan, *On Deconstruction: Theory and Criticism after Structuralism* (London, Melbourne and Henley, 1983).

Della Volpe, G., 'Settling accounts with the Russian Formalists', *New Left Review*, 113–14 (January–April 1979), 133–45.

Demetz, P., *Marx, Engels and the Poets* (Chicago, Ill., 1967).

Denning, Michael, 'Beggars and thieves: the ideology of the gang', *Literature and History*, 8 (1982), 41–55.

Derrida, Jacques, 'Structure, sign, and play in the discourse of the human sciences', in R. Macksey and E. Donato (eds), *The Structuralist Controversy* (Baltimore, Md. and London, 1970, 1972), pp. 247–72.

Derrida, Jacques, *Of Grammatology*, trans. Gayatri C. Spivak (Baltimore, Md. and London, 1976).

Donaldson, Ian, *The World Upside-Down. Comedy from Jonson to Fielding* (London, 1970).

Eagleton, Terry, *Criticism and Ideology: a Study in Marxist Literary Theory* (London, 1976).

Eagleton, Terry, 'The idealism of American criticism', *New Left Review*, 127 (May–June 1981a), 53–65.

Eagleton, Terry, *Walter Benjamin or Towards a Revolutionary Criticism* (London, 1981b).

Eco, Umberto, *The Role of the Reader: Explorations in the Semiotics of Texts* (London, Melbourne, Sydney, Auckland and Johannesburg, 1981).

Ehrenpreis, I, 'Personae', in C. Camden (ed.), *Restoration and Eighteenth-Century Literature* (Chicago, Ill., 1963), pp. 25–37.

Elias, Norbert, 'Problems of involvement and detachment', *British Journal of Sociology*, 7 (1956), 226–52.

Eliot, T. S., *Selected Essays* (3rd edn, London, 1951).

Ellmann, Richard, *Yeats the Man and the Masks* (London, 1961).

Ellmann, Richard, *Eminent Domain* (New York, 1967).

Empson, William, *Some Versions of Pastoral* (London, 1935, 1966).

Erlich, V., *Russian Formalism: History-Doctrine* (3rd edn, The Hague, 1969).

Ewald, W. B., *The Masks of Jonathan Swift* (Cambridge, Mass., 1954).

Felman, Shoshana, 'On reading poetry: reflections on the limits and possibilities of psychoanalytic approaches', in Joseph H. Smith (ed.), *The Literary Freud: Mechanisms of Defence and the Poetic Will* (New Haven, Conn. and London, 1980).

Feyerabend, Paul, 'How to be a good empiricist', in P. H. Nidditch (ed.), *The Philosophy of Science* (London, 1968), pp. 12–39.

Feyerabend, Paul, *Against Method* (London, 1977).

Feyerabend, Paul, *Science in a Free Society* (London, 1978).

Fish, Stanley, *Self-Consuming Artifacts: the Experience of Seventeenth-Century Literature* (Berkeley, Calif., 1972).

Fokkema, D. W. and Kunne-Ibsch, E., *Theories of Literature in the Twentieth Century. Structuralism, Marxism, Aesthetics of Reception, Semiotics* (London, 1977).

Forgacs, D., 'Marxist Literary Theories', in A. Jefferson and D. Robey (eds), *Modern Literary Theories* (London, 1982), pp. 134–69.

Foucault, Michel, *The Archaeology of Knowledge*, trans. A. M. Sheridan Smith (New York, 1972).

Foucault, Michel, *Language, Counter-Memory, Practice: Selected Essays and Interviews*, trans. D. F. Bouchard and S. Simon (Oxford, 1977).

Frye, Northrop, *Anatomy of Criticism: Four Essays* (Princeton, NJ, 1957).

Furst, L. R., *Romanticism in Perspective* (London, 1969).

Garaudy, Roger, *Marxism in the Twentieth Century*, trans. R. Hague (London, 1970).

Garrod, H. W., *Wordsworth: Lectures and Essays* (Oxford, 1927).

Garvin, Paul L. (ed.), *A Prague School Reader on Esthetics, Literary Structure, and Style* (Washington, 1964).

Gay, John, *The Beggar's Opera*, ed. P. E. Lewis (Edinburgh, 1973).

Gay, John, *Poetry and Prose*, (eds) V. A. Dearing and C. E. Beckwith, 2 vols (London, 1974).

Gray, Camilla, *The Great Experiment: Russian Art, 1863–1922* (London, 1962).

Gueunier, N., 'La production littéraire: métaphore, concept ou champ problématique?', *Littérature*, 14 (1974), 3–18.

Guillén, C., *Literature as System* (Princeton, NJ, 1971).

Hahn, Otto, 'Sartre's criticism', in R. Macksey (ed.), *Velocities of Change* (Baltimore, Md., 1974), pp. 260–76.

Hall, Stuart, 'Debate, psychology, ideology and the human subject', *Ideology and Consciousness*, 3 (1978), 113–21.

Handy, William J., *Kant and the Southern New Critics* (Austin, Tex., 1963).

Hay, Douglas, 'Property, authority and the criminal law', in Hay *et al.* (eds), *Albion's Fatal Tree, Crime and Society in Eighteenth-Century England* (London, 1975), pp. 17–63.

Hayes, C. W., 'Linguistics and literature: prose and poetry', in A. A. Hill (ed.), *Linguistics Today* (New York, 1969), pp. 173–87.

Hazlitt, William, *Complete Works*, 21 vols, ed. P. P. Howe (London, 1930–4).

Heath, Stephen, *The Nouveau Roman* (London, 1972).

Hirst, Paul, *On Law and Ideology* (London and Basingstoke, 1979).

Hyman, L., 'Indeterminacy in literary criticism', *Soundings*, 59 (1976), 345–56.

Iser, Wolfgang, *The Act of Reading. A Theory of Aesthetic Response* (London and Henley, 1978).

Jakobson, Roman, *The Framework of Language* (Michigan, 1980).

Jameson, F., *The Prison-House of Language: a Critical Account of Structuralism and Russian Formalism* (Princeton, NJ, 1971).

Jauss, Hans Robert, 'Literary history as a challenge to literary theory', *New Literary History*, 2 (1970), reprinted in Ralph Cohen (ed.), *New Directions in Literary History* (London, 1974), pp. 11–41.

Jenny, L., 'The strategy of form', in T. Todorov (ed.), *French Literary Theory Today*, trans. R. Carter (Cambridge, 1982).

Johnson, Barbara, 'Nothing fails like success', *SCE Reports*, 8 (1980), 7–16.

Johnson, Richard, 'Histories of culture/theories of ideology: notes on an impasse', in M. Barrett *et al.* (eds), *Ideology and Cultural Production* (London, 1979), pp. 49–77.

Johnson, Samuel, *The Works*, Yale edn (New Haven, Conn. and London, 1958–   ).

Kavanagh, James H., 'Marxism's Althusser: towards a politics of literary theory', *Diacritics*, 12 (1982), 25–45.

Kierkegaard, Søren, *The Point of View for My Work as an Author*, trans. W. Lowrie (London, 1939, 1962).

Kristeva, J., 'The ruin of poetics', in Bann and Bowlt (1973), pp. 102–21.

Kristeva, J., 'The system and the speaking subject', *Times Literary Supplement* (October 1973), 1249–50.

Kristeva, J., *La Révolution du langage poétique* (Paris, 1974).

Kuhn, T. S., *The Structure of Scientific Revolutions* (Chicago, Ill., 1962).

Kuhn, T. S., *The Essential Tension: Selected Studies in Scientific Tradition and Change* (Chicago, Ill. and London, 1977).

Lacan, Jacques, *Écrits, A Selection*, trans. A. Sheridan (London, 1977).

Laclau, Ernesto, *Politics and Ideology in Marxist Theory* (London, 1977).

Lakatos, I. and Musgrave, A., *Criticism and the Growth of Knowledge* (Cambridge, 1970).

Langbaum, Robert, *The Poetry of Experience. The Dramatic Monologue in Modern Literary Tradition* (1957, London, 1974).

Leatherdale, W. H., *The Role of Analogy, Model and Metaphor in Science* (Amsterdam, 1974).

Leavis, F. R., *The Great Tradition* (London, 1948, 1962).

Leavis, F. R., *The Common Pursuit* (London, 1952).

Lecourt, Dominique, *Proletarian Science? The Case of Lysenko*, trans. B. Brewster (London, 1977).

Lemaire, Anika, *Jacques Lacan*, trans. D. Macey (London, 1977).

Lemon, L. T. and Reis, M. J. (eds), *Russian Formalist Criticism: Four Essays* (Lincoln, Nebr., 1965).

Lentricchia, Frank, *After the New Criticism* (Chicago, Ill., 1980).

Lévi-Strauss, Claude, *The Savage Mind* (London, 1966).

Lifshitz, Mikhail, *The Philosophy of Art of Karl Marx*, trans. R. B. Winn (London, 1973).

Lillo, George, *The London Merchant*, ed. W. H. McBurney (London, 1965).

Lodge, David, *Language of Fiction* (London, 1966).

Lodge, David, *The Modes of Modern Writing: Metaphor Metonymy, and the Typology of Modern Literature* (London, 1977).

Loftis, John, *The Politics of Drama in Augustan England* (London, 1963).

MacCabe, Colin, *James Joyce and the Revolution of the Word* (London and Basingstoke, 1978).

MacCabe, Colin, 'On discourse', in MacCabe (ed.), *The Talking Cure: Essays in Psychoanalysis and Language* (London, 1981), pp. 188–217.

Macherey, Pierre, *A Theory of Literary Production*, trans. G. Wall (London, 1978, French original 1970).

Mack, Maynard, 'The muse of satire', *Yale Review*, 41 (1951), 80–92.

Macksey, R. and Donato, E. (eds), *The Structuralist Controversy: the Languages of Criticism and the Sciences of Man* (Baltimore, Md. and London, 1972).

Marx, K. and Engels, F., *Literature and Art: Selections from their Writings* (New York, 1947).

Marx, Karl, *Writings of the Young Marx on Philosophy and Society*, (eds) L. D. Easton and K. H. Guddat (New York, 1967).

Marx, Karl, *The German Ideology*, ed. C. J. Arthur (London, 1970).

Marx, Karl, *Grundrisse*, trans. M. Nicolaus (London, 1973).

Matejka, L. and Pomorska, K. (eds), *Readings in Russian Poetics: Formalist and Structuralist Views* (Ann Arbor, Mich., 1978).

Matejka, L., 'On the first Russian prologomena to semiotics', in Voloshinov (1973), pp. 161–74.

Michaels, Walter Benn, 'The interpreter's self: Pierce on the Cartesian "Subject"', in Tompkins (1980), pp. 185–200.

Mill, J. S., *On the Logic of the Moral Sciences*, ed. H. M. Magid (Indianapolis, 1965).

Mill, J. S., *Autobiography*, ed. J. Stillinger (Boston, Mass., 1969).

Mill, J. S., *Autobiography and Literary Essays*, (eds) J. M. Robson and J. Stillinger (Toronto and Buffalo, NY, 1981).

Miller, J. Hillis, *The Disappearance of God* (Cambridge, 1963).

Mitchell, S., 'From Shklovsky to Brecht: some preliminary remarks toward a history of the politicisation of Russian Formalism', *Screen*, 15, ii (1974), 74–81.

Monro, Thomas, 'The Marxist theory of art history', *Journal of Aesthetics and Art Criticism*, 4 (1961) 430–45.

Morawski, Stefan, 'The aesthetic views of Marx and Engels', *Journal of Aesthetics and Art Criticism*, 28 (1970), 301–4.

Mukařovský, Jan, *Aesthetic Function, Norm and Value as Social Facts*, trans. M. E. Suino (Ann Arbor, Mich., 1979).

Nietzsche, Friedrich, *The Will to Power*, trans. W. Kaufmann and R. J. Hollingdale (New York, 1967).

Noble, Yvonne (ed.), *Twentieth Century Interpretations of the Beggar's Opera* (Englewood Cliffs, NJ, 1975).

Norris, Christopher, *Deconstruction: Theory and Practice* (London and New York, 1982).

Olson, E., 'Rhetoric and the appreciation of Pope', *Modern Philology*, 37 (1939), 13–35, reprinted in E. P. J. Corbett (ed.), *Rhetorical Analyses of Literary Works* (London and Toronto, 1969), pp. 37–53.

Pike, C. (ed.), *The Futurists, the Formalists, and the Marxist Critique* (London, 1979).

Polyani, Michael, *Personal Knowledge: Towards a Post-Critical Philosophy* (Chicago, Ill., 1958).

Pomorska, K., *Russian Formalist Theory and its Poetic Ambiance* (The Hague, 1968).

Pope, Alexander, *The Poems*, one-volume Twickenham edn, ed. John Butt (London, 1963).

Pound, Ezra, *Gaudier-Brzeska: a Memoir* (London and New York, 1916).

Pound, Ezra, *Personae, Collected Shorter Poems* (London, 1952).

Pound, Ezra, *Literary Essays* (London, 1954).

Prawer, S. S., *Karl Marx and World Literature* (London, 1976).

Preston, John, 'The ironic mode: a comparison of *Jonathan Wild* and *The Beggar's Opera*', *Essays in Criticism*, 16 (1966), 268–80.

Putnam, Hilary, *Reason, Truth and History* (Cambridge, 1981).

Rader, Ralph W., 'Fact, theory and literary explanation', *Critical Inquiry*, 1 (1974), 245–72.

Reff, Theodore, *Degas, the Artist's Mind* (London, 1976).

Riffaterre, Michael, 'Describing poetic structures: two approaches to Baudelaire's "Les Chats"', in J. Ehrmann (ed.), *Structuralism* (Garden City, NY, 1970).

Rodway, Alan, *The Truths of Fiction* (London, 1970).

Russell, D. A. and Winterbottom, M., *Ancient Literary Criticism* (London, 1972).

Rycroft, Charles, *A Critical Dictionary of Psychoanalysis* (1968, London, 1972).

Said, Edward W., 'The text, the world, and the critic', in J. V. Harari (ed.), *Textual Strategies: Perspectives in Post-Structuralist Criticism* (London, 1980), 161–88.

Saussure, F. de, *Course in General Linguistics*, trans. W. Baskin, introd. by J. Culler (London, 1974).

Scheffler, Israel, *Science and Subjectivity* (Indianapolis, 1967).

Schilling, Bernard N., *Dryden and the Conservative Myth* (New Haven, Conn. and London, 1961).

Schleusener, Jay, 'Literary criticism and the philosophy of science', *Critical Inquiry*, 1 (1974), 892–900.

Schmidt, Siegfried J. 'Literary science as a science of argument', *New Literary History*, 7 (1976), 467–82.

Schultz, W. E., *Gay's Beggar's Opera. Its Content History & Influence* (New Haven, Conn., 1923).

Selden, Raman, 'Historical thought and Marvell's "Horatian Ode",' *Durham University Journal*, 65 (1972), 41–53.

Selden, Raman, 'Aesthetics and criticism: against a division of labour', *British Journal of Aesthetics*, 15 (1975), 69–80.

Selden, Raman, *English Verse Satire, 1590–1765* (London, 1978).

Sheridan, Alan, *Michel Foucault. The Will to Truth* (London and New York, 1980).

Sherwood, R., 'Translations from *Lef* with an Introduction', *Screen*, 12, iv (1971/2), 25–58.

Sherwood, R., 'Victor Shklovsky and the development of early Formalist theory on prose literature', in Bann and Bowlt (1973), pp. 26–40.

Sherwood, R., 'Mayakovsky, formalism and revolution', *Essays in Poetics*, 3, i (1978), 83–106.

Sharratt, Bernard, *Reading Relations: Structures of Literary Production: A Dialectical Text/Book* (Brighton, Sussex, 1981).

Silverman, David and Torode, Brian, *The Material Word: Some Theories of Language and its Limits* (London, Boston, Mass. and Henley, 1980).

Slatoff, Walter J., *With Respect to Readers: Dimensions of Literary Response* (Ithaca, NY, 1970).

Spivak, Gayatri, translator's preface, in Derrida, *Of Grammatology* (Baltimore, Md. and London, 1976).

Stacy, R. H., *Russian Literary Criticism: a Short History* (Syracuse, NY, 1974).

Stern, J. P., *Nietzsche* (London, 1978).

Suleiman, Susan R. and Crosman, Inge (eds), *The Reader in the Text* (Princeton, NJ, 1980).

Taylor, R., 'The Marxist theory of art', *Radical Philosophy*, 5 (1973), 29–34.

Therborn, Goran, *The Ideology of Power and the Power of Ideology* (London, 1980).

Thompson, E. P., *Whigs and Hunters: the Origin of the Black Act* (London, 1975).

Thompson, E. W., *Russian Formalism and Anglo-American New Criticism* (The Hague, 1971).

Titunik, I. R., 'The formal method and the sociological method in Russian theory and study of literature', in Voloshinov (1973), pp. 175–200.

Tompkins, Jane P. (ed.), *Reader-Response Criticism: from Formalism to Post-Structuralism* (Baltimore, Md. and London, 1980).

Trotsky, L., *Literature and Revolution*, trans. R. Strunsky (Ann Arbor, Mich., 1960).

Valéry, Paul, *Degas Manet Morisot*, trans. D. Paul (New York, 1960).

Viner, Jacob, 'Satire and economics in the Augustan age of satire', in H. K. Miller *et al.* (eds), *The Augustan Milieu: Essays Presented to L. A. Landa* (London, 1970), pp. 77–101.

Voloshinov, V. N., *Marxism and the Philosophy of Language*, trans. L. Matejka and I. R. Titunik (New York and London, 1973).

Wasiolek, E., 'Texts are made and not given: a response to a critique', *Critical Inquiry*, 2 (1975), 386–91.

Werckmeister, O. K., 'Marx on ideology and art', *New Literary History*, 2 (1973), 501–19.

Wesker, Arnold, *The Wesker Trilogy* (Penguin edn, London, 1964).

White, Hayden, *Tropics of Discourse, Essays in Cultural Criticism* (Baltimore, Md. and London, 1978).

Whitehead, A. N., *Science and the Modern World* (Cambridge, 1926).

Wilde, Oscar, *Essays*, ed. H. Pearson (London, 1950).

Williams, Raymond, *Culture and Society 1780–1950* (London, 1958, 1963).

Williams, Raymond, *The Long Revolution* (London, 1961, 1965).

Williams, Raymond, *Marxism and Literature* (London, 1977).

Winterbourne, A. T., 'Objectivity in science and aesthetics', *British Journal of Aesthetics*, 21 (1981), 253–60.

Wollen, P., '"Ontology" and "materialism" in film', *Screen*, 17, i (1976), 7–25.

Wright, G. T., *The Poet in the Poem: the Personae of Eliot, Yeats and Pound* (Berkeley, Calif. and London, 1960).

Young, Robert (ed.), *Untying the Text: a Post-Structuralist Reader* (Boston, Mass., London and Henley, 1981).

Index